EFFECTIVE WRITING

THIRD EDITION

EFFECTIVE WRITING
A Handbook
for Accountants

Claire May, Ph.D.
University of South Alabama

 PRENTICE HALL, *Englewood Cliffs, NJ 07632*

Library of Congress of Cataloging-in-Publication Data

May, Claire
    Effective writing : a handbook for accountants / Claire May. — 3rd
ed.
        p.   cm.
    Includes index.
    ISBN: 0-13-244864-5
    1. Business report writing.   2. Communication in accounting.
    I. Title.
    HF5719.M375   1992
    808'.066657—dc20   91-29067
                                                            CIP

Acquisition editor: Terri Daly
Production editor: Susan E. Rowan
Cover design: 20/20 Services, Inc.
Prepress buyer: Trudy Pisciotti
Manufacturing buyer: Bob Anderson

 © 1992, 1989, 1984 by Prentice-Hall, Inc.
A Paramount Communications Company
Englewood Cliffs, New Jersey 07632

Printed in the United States of America
10   9   8   7

ISBN: 0-13-244864-5

Prentice-Hall International (UK) Limited, *London*
Prentice-Hall of Australia Pty. Limited, *Sydney*
Prentice-Hall Canada Inc., *Toronto*
Prentice-Hall Hispanoamericana, S.A., *Mexico*
Prentice-Hall of India Private Limited, *New Delhi*
Prentice-Hall of Japan, Inc., *Tokyo*
Simon & Schuster Asia Pte. Ltd., *Singapore*
Editora Prentice-Hall do Brasil, Ltda., *Rio de Janeiro*

CONTENTS

3

THE FLOW OF THOUGHT
Organizing for Coherence   24

4

A SENSE OF STYLE
Writing with Conciseness and Clarity   47

5

STANDARD ENGLISH
Grammar, Punctuation, and Spelling   73

6

FORMAT FOR CLARITY
Document Design   *94*

Part II   BUSINESS DOCUMENTS

7

LETTERS   *101*

8

MEMOS   *128*

9

REPORTS   *148*

10

RESEARCH PAPERS   *174*

Part III   ORAL PRESENTATIONS

11

ORAL PRESENTATIONS
Preparation   *184*

12

MAKING THE PRESENTATION
Poise and Confidence   *192*

APPENDICES

APPENDIX A

APPENDIX B

PREFACE

Effective Writing: A Handbook for Accountants, 3rd Edition, is designed to help accounting students and practitioners improve their communication skills. It can be used as a supplementary text for regular accounting courses, as a text in an accounting communication course, or as a text in a business communication or technical writing course when these courses include accounting students. The handbook is also a useful desk reference or self-study manual for accounting professionals.

Effective Writing guides the writer through all the stages of the writing process: planning, including analysis of audience and purpose; generating and organizing ideas; writing the draft; revising for readable style and correct grammar; and designing the document for effective presentation. In addition to these basic writing principles, the book includes chapters on letters, memos, reports, and other formats used by accountants in actual practice, plus a new appendix on writing for the CPA exam. Throughout the text, *Effective Writing* stresses coherence, conciseness, and clarity as the most important qualities of the writing done by professional accountants.

Also new in this edition are two chapters on oral presentations. The first chapter discusses preparation of the presentation, including audience analysis and organization of materials, and the second covers techniques of effective delivery.

Included in the chapters of *Effective Writing* are exercises and assignments that reinforce the concepts covered in the text. Some exercises have answers, for independent review. Other exercises without answers also appear in the text, with answers in the new Instructor's Manual. Most chapters also contain topics for writing or speaking assignments. These assignments, like the illustrations in the text, deal with accounting concepts and situations, and thus will seem more relevant and interesting to men and women involved in the study and practice of accounting. Communication topics are keyed to the accounting courses for which they might be most suitable as class assignments.

One way to use *Effective Writing* is in conjunction with regular accounting courses. Instructors can assign cases and topics for research based on the accounting concepts actually being studied in class, or use the assignments provided in this handbook. Students then analyze the accounting problem, research the literature if necessary, and prepare their answers according to an assigned format such as a letter, technical memo, formal report, or oral presentation. The handbook will guide the students toward principles of effective writing and speaking. Instructors can then evaluate students' performance based on the criteria discussed in the text and the Instructor's Manual.

The Instructor's Manual is new for this edition. It contains suggestions for everyone wishing to improve the communication skills of accounting students, whether in a regular accounting course or in a course devoted to communication. The Manual contains suggestions on such topics as motivating students to improve their communication skills, designing assignments, and evaluating performance. The Manual also contains chapter commentaries and masters for transparencies and handouts.

As a self-study manual, *Effective Writing* will help accounting professionals master the techniques of successful writing in the business world. The book contains numerous examples and practical applications of the techniques discussed. In addition, some chapters have self-test exercises, with answers, which will enable the reader to practice the principles. A thoughtful review of *Effective Writing,* then, will give practicing accountants greater confidence in the writing situations that they encounter as part of their professional responsibilities.

The handbook covers the writing and speaking problems most frequently encountered by accounting students and practitioners, as demonstrated by extensive classroom testing and research into the communication needs of the profession. It is my hope that this book will help both those preparing to enter the profession and those already in practice to achieve greater success through effective communication.

I wish to thank all the people who have helped me prepare this book, especially Gordon S. May, Evelyn S. Lapp, Ben T. Beasley, Anna Marie Soper, Billie Sanders, Susan E. Rowan, and Terri Daly.

Claire May

1

ACCOUNTANTS AS COMMUNICATORS

Most accountants are concerned about the need for effective writing skills. Multinational accounting firms offer special courses to help their accountants write better. Various accounting organizations—the AICPA and state societies, for example— offer continuing education courses in writing. Many colleges and universities now stress effective writing in accounting coursework.[1]

Why all this interest in writing? To be truly competent, accountants must be able to use words effectively.

The managing partners of the nation's largest public accounting firms have issued a paper that stresses the importance of communication skills to the successful practice of accounting:

> Public accounting requires its practitioners to be able to transfer and receive information with ease. Practitioners must be able to present and defend their views through formal and informal, written and oral, presentation. They must be able to do so at a peer level with business executives.... Practitioners must be able to listen effectively to gain information and understand opposing points of view. They also will need the ability to locate, obtain and organize information from both human and electronic sources.[2]

The American Accounting Association's Committee to Prepare a Statement of Basic Accounting Theory also identified the importance of communication in the practice of accounting: "Communication is a vital link in accounting activity. It is of no less importance than that of developing the information itself."[3]

So the ability to communicate effectively—whether in speaking or writing—is essential to success in the accounting profession.

Unfortunately, many students and accountants lack the basic skills they need to be effective communicators. *The Wall Street Journal* has reported that as many as one-third of the accounting firms surveyed are dissatisfied with the communication skills of entry-level accountants.[4] In another study to determine why entry-level accountants lose their jobs, a high percentage of firms reported poor writing skills as a major reason for job terminations.[5]

Because the ability to communicate effectively plays an important part in an accountant's success on the job, many employers screen prospective accountants for adequate skills in oral and written communication. In fact, one study shows communication skills to be the most important factor in decisions to hire new accountants. Employers view the ability to write and speak effectively as even more important than a prospective employee's grade point average.[6]

So accountants need good communication skills to get a good job in the first place and to keep that job after they're hired. Of course "communication skills" is a broad area. It includes formal and informal oral presentations, interpersonal communication, reading, listening, and many other skills as well. But since this book is primarily about writing, let's look further at some of the kinds of documents accountants write on the job.

WHAT DO ACCOUNTANTS WRITE?

No matter what kind of practice accountants have, writing is an essential part of the job. Whether in public accounting, management accounting, not-for-profit accounting, or governmental accounting, and whether specializing in tax, auditing, systems, or some other area, accountants write every day.

Examples in three areas, tax, auditing, and systems, will suggest a few of the many occasions that require accountants to write. A tax accountant often writes memos to describe to other members of the firm the results of his or her research. These memos become part of the clients' files. Then the accountant may write letters to the clients advising them about the best way to handle their tax problems. Often tax accountants must also write letters to the Internal Revenue Service on behalf of clients.

Auditors write memos describing the work done on an audit to be filed with the audit working papers. Auditors may also write memos to their colleagues to request advice or to report research results. Following the audit engagement, auditors often write advisory letters to management of the audited firm; the purpose of these letters is to suggest ways to improve accounting and internal control procedures.

Systems specialists might write documents for readers with varying degrees of computer expertise. For example, they might write a user primer to explain in elementary terms how to use a certain software package. Or they might write a highly technical report on a complex accounting system application.

No matter what their specialty, all accountants write memos to their supervisors, subordinates, and coworkers to request or provide information. They also write letters to clients, agencies, and a variety of other readers.

Reports, both formal and informal, are also important ways accountants communicate. For instance, an accountant working for a corporation may write a report for management on alternative accounting treatments for a particular business transaction.

To be effective, letters, memos, and reports must be well written. How will clients react if, after reading a letter from their CPA, they are still confused about their income tax problem? How will management feel about a report that is poorly organized and hard to follow?

Accountants may also write the narrative portions of financial statements. For instance, footnote disclosures communicate information that users may need to interpret the statements accurately. Here is an example of a footnote disclosure in the 1989 annual report of Coca-Cola (Reproduced with Permission of the Coca-Cola Company):

> **5. Short-term Borrowings and Credit Arrangements.** Loans and notes payable consist of commercial paper and notes payable to banks and other financial institutions.
>
> Under lines of credit and other credit facilities for short-term debt with various financial institutions, the Company may borrow up to $925 million. These lines of credit are subject to normal banking terms and conditions. At December 31, 1989, the unused portion of the credit lines was $837 million, of which $605 million was available to support commercial paper borrowings. Some of the financial arrangements require compensating balances which are not material.[7]

This footnote is fairly easy to understand. Unfortunately, the meaning of some footnote disclosures is not always clear to the average financial statement reader. Arthur Adelberg and Richard Lewis, in an article in the *Journal of Accountancy,* note the need for more clearly written footnotes. They suggest, for instance, that accountants use shorter sentences, active verbs, and definitions of technical terms when writing footnotes and other narrative portions of financial statements.[8]*

HOW WELL DO ACCOUNTANTS WRITE?

The answer to this question—how well accountants write—has already been suggested by the study reporting the large numbers of entry-level accountants who lose their jobs because of poor writing skills. And some employers believe the

*Copyright © 1980 by the American Institute of Certified Public Accountants.

problem is getting worse. One study suggests that almost half of all Big Six practitioners believe that writing skills of their newly hired staff have declined in the last few years.[9]

A letter to *The Wall Street Journal* points out the high costs to employers when their accounting employees lack adequate writing skills, including the costs of quality control measures to correct faulty writing. In addition, "The expense of hiring and training those who are subsequently fired for [poor writing ability] must surely represent a tremendous waste of resources."[10]

In a study sponsored by the American Accounting Association, Robert W. Ingram and Charles R. Frazier identified 20 communication skills important to the successful practice of accounting. A disturbing finding of the study was that *entry-level staff and accounting students are woefully deficient in most of these skills.*[11]

Of the skills identified by Ingram and Frazier, the following relate directly or indirectly to effective writing:

- correspondence writing
- memorandums and informal report writing
- formal report writing
- correct grammar
- correct punctuation
- correct spelling
- outline development
- inductive reasoning
- deductive reasoning
- coherence
- clarity
- conciseness
- paragraph development
- use of visual aids[12]

It is the purpose of this book to help you improve these very important writing skills, whether you're preparing to enter the accounting profession or you're already on the job.

WHAT MAKES WRITING WORK?

Ingram and Frazier's list of writing skills suggests some of the qualities of effective writing. Three of these qualities—coherence, clarity, and conciseness—summarize the others on the list.

Coherence is the logical, orderly relationship of ideas. Coherent writing is, quite simply, writing that is well organized. The flow of thought is easy to follow and important ideas stand out. For your writing to be coherent, you must carefully think through the ideas you wish to convey. The ideas must be arranged logically and then written in a way readers will be able to understand.

Clarity means that the writing is written as simply as possible, using words and phrases with which the reader is familiar. To improve the clarity of your writing, choose words that mean precisely what you intend so that your sentences convey only one meaning: the meaning you intend to convey. The use of standard English—correct grammar, punctuation, and spelling—also contributes to clear writing.

Conciseness means that you say what needs to be said in as few words as possible. To keep your writing concise, avoid digressions, unnecessary repetition, and a wordy style.

Coherence, clarity, and conciseness: these are three important qualities of effective writing, qualities that make the writing work. You can use a number of strategies to achieve these qualities. For example, you can plan your writing and revise your documents so that the final drafts are polished and correct. You should also keep in mind two concerns that are basic to effective writing—the purpose of the document you are writing and the needs and expectations of the readers. In fact, thinking often about a document's purpose and readers will help ensure that your writing is coherent, clear, and concise.

YOU CAN BECOME A GOOD WRITER

With all this talk about the importance of good writing to a successful career in accounting, you may be feeling overwhelmed or even discouraged. Many people believe they can never become good writers.

A word of encouragement is in order. The truth is that virtually anyone who succeeds in college work has the education and the ability to become at least an adequate writer, and probably even a good one. Problems with writing are often the result of two factors, both of which can be corrected: a lack of adequate training in writing skills and a lack of self-confidence.

Let's address the latter problem, the poor self-image some people have of themselves as writers.

One reason to be optimistic about your writing ability is that you already know quite a bit about how to write. You've acquired writing skills in English and other writing classes, as well as from your own experience. Most people are better writers than they realize. They have the potential to become even more effective after they've mastered a few strategies such as the ones we'll cover in this book. As you read upcoming chapters, note the techniques and principles that you already use in your writing. Don't lose sight of your strengths while you work to improve those areas that could be better.

Another reason you should be able to write well as an accountant is that you will be writing about topics that you understand and find interesting. If you have had unpleasant experiences with writing in courses other than accounting, the problem may have been that you were writing about topics you weren't particularly interested in or qualified to discuss. When we write about subjects we like and understand, it's much easier to write with clarity and persuasion.

Finally, you may find it much easier to do the kind of writing recommended in this book because it will be simple, direct writing. Some people believe they must write in long, complicated sentences filled with difficult, "impressive" vocabulary. In fact, just the opposite is true: effective business writing, including that done by accountants, is written as simply as possible. It is thus easier to do.

WRITING AND OTHER FORMS
OF COMMUNICATION

We mentioned earlier that writing is only one of several forms of communication, along with such skills as speaking, reading, listening, and interpersonal communication. In fact, all of these forms of communication are interactive: they work together to determine how well a person gives and receives information. Let's look at how reading, listening, and speaking skills can help you improve your writing.[13]

Reading

Reading affects writing in several ways. Often you will write a memo or letter in response to a written communication from someone else. If you are in public practice, for example, you may write a letter to clients to answer questions they have posed in a letter to your firm. The ability to read the earlier correspondence carefully is essential to an effective response.

Careful reading is also important when you research accounting literature as background for the documents you write. The tax code, government regulations, Financial Accounting Standards Board pronouncements, and articles in professional journals are examples of the material you must read to stay informed on accounting issues and procedures. You will need to understand this material and be able to apply it to particular situations within your own company or those of your clients.

You will also read information circulated and stored within your own firm or company, such as client files and memos from colleagues. Reading this material carefully will provide you with many of the insights and facts you need to deal effectively with situations for which you're responsible.

Thus careful reading, with an understanding of important ideas and key facts, can contribute to effective writing.

Listening

Along with reading, the ability to listen carefully determines how well you receive information from others. On the job you may interact with colleagues, supervisors, subordinates, or clients; at school you also interact with professors and other students. Listening carefully to these people will provide you with important information you can use as the basis of your writing. It will provide you with facts about projects you are working on, along with insights into other people's expectations and concerns.

We can think of many situations when listening skills contribute to effective writing: instructions given by the professor in class, interviews with clients, requests from supervisors, and phone conversations with colleagues are a few examples. In all these situations, attentive listening is necessary to hear what people are saying. It's often a good idea to take notes and, when necessary, to ask questions for clarification or additional information.

Careful listening to what others say is often a key ingredient in effective writing. When you listen carefully, you will learn much about what others know about a situation, what their concerns are, and what they expect from you.

Speaking

What you write will also affect what you say to others. Informally, you may have meetings and conversations to discuss reports or memos you've written, for example.

What you write may also be the basis for formal oral presentations. You might make a presentation to a board of directors, senior managers, or members of a professional organization.

WRITING AND PROBLEM SOLVING

In the introduction to this chapter, we saw that the nation's largest public accounting firms are unanimous in calling for improved communication skills for those entering the profession. In the same paper in which they talk about the importance of communication, these firms also identify problem-solving skills as essential to successful accounting practice:

> Individuals seeking to be successful in the diverse world of public accounting must be able to use creative problem-solving skills in a consultative process. They must be able to solve diverse and unstructured problems in unfamiliar settings. They must be able to comprehend an unfocused set of facts; identify and, if possible, anticipate problems; and find acceptable solutions.[14]

Problem solving requires many skills, such as the identification of key issues, research into relevant literature, and the ability to think critically and analytically. At each step of the problem-solving process, the writing you do can help you reach sound conclusions.

You can generate ideas on a topic if you write down what you know on that topic, as well as what you have yet to find out. The act of writing about a subject can actually help you clarify your thinking. As one wit has put it: "How do I know what I think till I see what I say?" There's more truth in this quip than might at first be apparent. Research into how people think and learn has shown that writers often generate ideas and improve their insights into a subject as they write down their thoughts.[15]

Writing can help you solve problems in other ways as well. For example, as you research accounting literature, you take notes. You may also write requests to other people for additional information you need in order to solve the problem.

The writing you do to solve problems is writing for yourself. Once the problems have been solved—or at least clearly defined—you can then put your insights and conclusions into writing that will help others.

Writing and problem solving, then, are often inseparable, interactive processes. Both are essential to the successful practice of accounting.

In conclusion, remember that accounting is a process of measuring and *communicating* information. Accountants need writing skills for many of their routine, professional tasks, whether communicating with investors, management, clients, or fellow professionals. They need to use words effectively and to combine these words into good sentences and paragraphs.

Communication skills pay off in professional advancement. Zane Robbins, of Arthur Andersen & Co., notes:

> All other things being equal, the professional accountant who can communicate best is likely to progress fastest. Those who are unable to write and communicate effectively often find themselves consigned to the purgatory of technician with little hope for long-term growth.[16]

To be a successful accountant, you must master many skills. You must understand and be able to apply accounting principles, of course, but you must also be able to communicate effectively. A competent accountant who is also an effective communicator will usually be rewarded with professional success.

EXERCISES

Exercise 1-1

Look for examples of effective and ineffective writing in the material you read regularly. Consider letters and memos you receive, as well as published professional material such as textbooks, professional articles, and FASB pronouncements. Then think about the following questions:

1. What kind of material do you find easiest to read? What are some of the qualities that make this writing readable?
2. Examine closely the writing you find difficult to read. How do you think the writing could be improved?
3. Make two lists of the specific qualities that make writing effective or ineffective. You might begin with these qualities:

EFFECTIVE WRITING	**INEFFECTIVE WRITING**

- conversational, everyday vocabulary
- main ideas easy to identify; writing gets to the point quickly
- correct grammar and spelling
- short paragraphs
- concise
- etc.

- jargon and "big words"
- rambling, unorganized; writing fails to get to the point quickly
- obvious grammatical and spelling mistakes
- long paragraphs
- longer than it needs to be
- etc.

Exercise 1–2

Collect samples of your own writing. Analyze your writing, considering the following questions:

1. What kind of response do you usually get to your writing from your supervisors, peers, clients, and subordinates? Are readers sometimes uncertain of your meaning?
2. From the lists you made for Exercise 1–1, question 3, identify some of the strengths and weaknesses of your writing.
3. Write a two-paragraph analysis of your writing. The first paragraph should identify the qualities of your writing that make it effective; the second paragraph should discuss what you need to improve.

   Begin each paragraph with a topic sentence that states the main idea of the paragraph. For example, the first paragraph could begin this way:

   My writing is effective in several ways. For example,...

Exercise 1–3

Assume you are a staff accountant in a CPA firm. One of the firm's partners, Elaine Peters, has complimented you on the memos you have written. However, Ms. Peters has noticed that some of the firm's other staff accountants do not write very good memos; nor do they believe that effective writing is important.

Write a memo to the other staff accountants in your firm. Discuss why well-written memos are important, and suggest some qualities that make the writing effective. Be sure that your own memo illustrates those qualities.

You will find suggestions on how to write a memo in Chapter 8.

NOTES

1. Gordon S. May and Claire B. May, "Communication Instruction: What Is Being Done to Develop the Communication Skills of Accounting Students?", *Journal of Accounting Education,* 7 (Fall 1989), pp. 233–44.
2. Duane R. Kullburg, William L. Gladstone, Peter R. Scanlon, J. Michael Cook, Ray J. Groves, Larry D. Horner, Shaun F. O'Malley, and Edward A. Kangas, *Perspectives on Education: Capabilities for Success in the Accounting Profession,* April 1989, p. 6.
3. Committee to Prepare a Statement of Basic Accounting Theory, *A Statement of Basic Accounting Theory* (Evanston, Ill.: American Accounting Association, 1966), p. 13.
4. "Words Count," *The Wall Street Journal,* July 16, 1986, p. 1.

5. Alan A. Cherry and Lucy A. Wilson, "A Study of the Writing Skills of Accounting Majors in California" (unpublished study, 1987).
6. "Popularity Poll Results," *New Accountant,* September 1986, p. 20.
7. The Coca-Cola Company, "Notes to Consolidated Financial Statements," *1989 Annual Report,* p. 51.
8. Arthur Harris Adelberg and Richard A. Lewis, "Financial Reports Can Be Made More Understandable," *Journal of Accountancy,* 149 (June 1980): 44–50.
9. Daniel P. Murphy, "An Analysis of the Application Skills Needed by Undergraduate Accounting Students Planning to Enter Tax Practice in the Southeastern United States: A Practitioner's Perspective," *Collected Papers of the American Accounting Association's Southeast Regional Meeting* (Atlanta, 1987), p. 120.
10. Gordon S. May, "No Accounting for Poor Writers," *The Wall Street Journal,* Letter to the Editor, May 29, 1987, p. 27.
11. Robert W. Ingram and Charles R. Frazier, *Developing Communications Skills for the Accounting Profession* (Evanston, Ill.: American Accounting Association, 1980).
12. Ibid., pp. 15–18.
13. Elizabeth E. Orem and Jane O. Burns, "The Problems and Challenges of Teaching Accounting Students to Communicate," *Georgia Journal of Accounting,* Spring 1988, pp. 9–24.
14. Kullburg, et al., p. 6.
15. Lee Odell, "The Process of Writing and the Process of Learning," *College Composition and Communication,* February 1980, pp. 41–50.
16. H. Zane Robbins, "How to Develop Basic Writing Skills," *The Chronicle,* 40, no. 1 (1981), 9.

2

THE WRITING PROCESS
An Overview

Effective writing, like accounting, is a process. The first step in the accounting process is to analyze the transactions to determine how they should be recorded. For example, the accountant decides where to record the transactions—what journals, ledgers, and accounts to use—and how detailed the entry description must be in order to be useful.

Several questions basic to the accounting system underlie an accountant's analysis of financial transactions and their treatment. What is the purpose of the information recorded and ultimately reported? Who are the users of this information and what are their needs? Do the readers expect this information to be presented in a certain form, such as the typical presentations found in annual reports? How can the information be most fairly and effectively presented?

These questions are as important to good writing as they are to good accounting. Initial planning, emphasizing both the purpose of the writing and the needs and expectations of the readers, is the first step in the writing process.

This chapter will discuss the writing process from beginning to end: planning for purpose and audience, gathering information, generating and organizing ideas, drafting, revising, and proofreading. It will then show you how to apply this process to overcome much of the anxiety you may feel about writing, including the problem of writer's block. Throughout the chapter, we will also discuss how computers, especially word processors, can help you at every stage of the writing process.

GETTING STARTED:
ANALYZING THE PROBLEM

The first stage in the writing process, analyzing the purpose of what you are to write, is easy to overlook. When you think about purpose, you decide what you want to accomplish with your letter, memo, or other document. Do you want to provide your readers with information about some topic, answer their questions, recommend a course of action? Persuade them to do something or agree with you on some point?

These are just a few of the purposes a document can have. What is important, however, is that you think carefully about the purpose *before* you begin to write. It might be helpful to think of purpose in terms of three categories: to give information about something, to propose a course of action, or to solve a problem. The purpose of most writing tasks will fall into one of these categories or perhaps a combination of two or three.

A report on inventory flow assumptions, for example, could have numerous purposes. If you were writing such a report, you would first decide on its primary purpose. Should the report simply describe the various flow assumptions—LIFO, FIFO, average cost, etc.? Is the purpose of the report to recommend an inventory accounting treatment for a certain company in a given situation? Should the report analyze the potential problems arising from a change in flow assumptions—from FIFO to LIFO, perhaps?

Here is another example. Assume you are the controller for Eldorado Manufacturing. Eldorado is considering a purchase of stock from Western Materials, one of Eldorado's major suppliers of raw materials. A report on this possible purchase could have any of the following purposes:

- To inform management of the advantages (or disadvantages) of such a purchase
- To recommend that Eldorado purchase (or not purchase) the stock
- To suggest a way to finance the purchase

The purpose of the report, or of any writing, will determine what material it should contain. Consider another example. Your client is faced with a lawsuit that could result in a large loss. You might write a letter to the client about the disclosure requirements for the contingent loss liability due to pending litigation. In such a letter you would not discuss gain contingencies, nor loss contingencies from bad debts. You would analyze the specific purpose of the letter to decide what information was relevant for this situation.

Another way to think about the purpose of a document is to identify the accounting issues you will be addressing. Sometimes these issues are obvious, but at other times you will need to analyze the situation carefully before all the issues become apparent. For example, a client may seek your help on the best way to record a transaction to minimize the income tax liability. As you analyze the transaction, you may become aware of accounting issues that would never occur to the client, such as the need to record the transaction consistently with generally accepted accounting principles.

Identifying the issues may help you to define the purposes of the document you are writing, since one purpose may be to explain the accounting issues in a way your reader can understand.

Once you have analyzed your purposes carefully, it's a good idea to write them down. Be as specific as possible, and try to define your purpose within one sentence. This sentence may later become part of the introduction of your letter, memo, or report.

Two final words about purpose: *be specific.* Remember that you are writing to particular individuals in a particular situation. Relate the purpose of your writing to these people and their concerns. That is, state the purpose in the context of this specific situation, rather than in broad, general terms. In the Eldorado Manufacturing example, suppose you were writing a report on how to finance a purchase of Western Materials stock. You would limit your discussion to the financing alternatives available to Eldorado and those practical for it to consider.

Sometimes to determine the purpose of a document you will need to read previous correspondence on the subject, such as a letter from a client. Be sure to read this correspondence carefully, underlining important information and noting what questions you've been asked to address in your response. You may also be asked orally to write something, perhaps by your supervisor. If you receive an oral request to write, listen carefully to the directions. If the purpose of the document is not clear, ask questions until you're sure what the document should include.

ANALYZING THE READERS

Another important consideration in the planning of a writing task is who the reader(s) will be. A memo on a highly technical accounting topic would be written one way for a fellow accountant, but another way for a client or manager with only limited knowledge of accounting procedures and terminology.

Effective writers analyze the needs and expectations of their readers before they begin to write. If you are writing a letter or memo, you will likely be writing to a limited number of people, perhaps to only one person. Furthermore, you usually know, or can find out, important information about the readers. Again, you must ask certain basic questions. How much knowledge do the readers have of the subject being discussed? The answer to this question will suggest the terms that should be defined, the procedures that should be explained, or the background information that should be provided.

Accountants dealing with the public should be particularly careful in analyzing the needs of their readers. For example, a tax specialist might have clients with widely varying experience and knowledge of taxation terminology. A corporation executive would probably understand such concepts as depreciation and accruals, but a small shopkeeper might not be familiar with these technical accounting terms and procedures. Business letters to these two clients, even on the same topic, would be written differently.

You should also consider the readers' attitudes and biases. Are they likely to be neutral to your recommendations, or will they need to be convinced? Remember to write with the readers' interests, needs, and concerns in mind. How will the readers benefit, directly or indirectly, from what you propose? How can you present your arguments so that readers' objections and biases will be overcome? To answer this last question you will need to anticipate readers' questions, research the basic issues, and then organize your arguments into a convincing sequence.

Other important considerations when analyzing readers' needs and expectations are tone and style. Again, what are their attitudes and biases? Some readers react well to an informal, friendly style of writing, but other readers believe that professional writing should be more formal. But whoever your readers are, remember always to be courteous. Whether you write in a technical or simplified style, all readers appreciate (and deserve!) consideration, tact, and respect.

Word choices also contribute to an effective writing style. Would some of your readers resent the following sentence?

> An efficient accountant dictates letters to his secretary; she then types the letters for his signature.

Some readers might argue that the choice of pronouns (accountant/he, secretary/she) implies a gender bias. This sentence can be revised to avoid the issue of gender bias by using plural nouns:

> Efficient accountants dictate letters to their secretaries, who then type the letters for their supervisors' signatures.

Sometimes your readers will have additional expectations about your documents that you should consider. In a classroom situation, for example, your instructor will usually give you directions for your papers, such as length, format, and due date. The instructor expects you to follow these directions; how well you do so will usually affect your grade.

Readers' expectations will also be important when you write on the job. For example, managers in some corporations expect in-house memos and reports to follow certain conventions of format, organization, or style. If you work for such a company, your memos and reports will seem more professional, and be more effective, if they are consistent with these expectations.

In fact, readers' expectations may actually be a matter of company or firm policy. Policies may govern how certain documents are written, or the procedures they must go through for approval. For instance, many public accounting firms will not let new staff send letters to clients unless they are first approved by a manager or partner. If you were a new staff member in such a firm, you might first draft the client letter, but the partner would expect to review it and possibly ask you to make revisions. Moreover, for certain documents, such as some engagement letters or audit reports, the actual language used in the letter might be determined by firm policy. The partner will expect you to follow these policies with great care.

It may have occurred to you that in the example of the client letter just discussed there are actually two readers: the partner who will review and approve the letter and the client who will be the ultimate recipient. This letter should be written on a technical level that is appropriate for the client, and it should address the client's concerns. Yet the letter should also meet the expectations of the partner. Analyzing readers' needs, interests, and expectations is obviously more complex in situations like this where there are several readers. You will need to think carefully about the different readers and use your best judgment to meet the expectations of them all.

Analyzing reader needs and expectations is an important part of the preparation for writing. Initial planning, which considers both your audience and your purpose, is the first rule of effective writing.

1.   **Analyze the purpose of the writing and the needs and expectations of the readers.**

GETTING YOUR IDEAS TOGETHER

Once you have evaluated the purpose of the writing and the needs of the readers, you are ready for the second stage in the writing process: gathering information and organizing the ideas you want to present. This step may be quick and simple. For a short letter that you can write without further research, organizing your ideas may involve only a short list of the main ideas you wish to include in the letter, perhaps one idea for each paragraph.

For much of the writing you do, however, gathering information and organizing may be a more complicated process, one involving a great deal of thought on your part, and perhaps some research as well. Let's look at some techniques you can use.

Gathering Information

Before you begin to write the document, be sure that you have all the information you need and that this information is accurate. Two useful ways to gather this information are to check the work that has already been done and to find out new information for yourself.

For many projects you'll be involved with, there may already be some information available. If you're working on an audit, for example, you may have information available from other members of the audit team as well as the files from the previous years' audits. Explore these sources of information fully: review the files carefully and, when necessary, talk with the people who have already worked on the project.

Sometimes you may also need to do additional research of your own. This may involve background reading on a technical topic or a careful review of accounting pronouncements, such as FASB statements or the Internal Revenue Code. As you read this material, take notes carefully and be alert for information that will help you when you write.

Your research may also require you to interview people who will be affected by the project you're working on. Suppose you're writing a report that will propose a new accounting information system for your company. You can gain important insights into topics your report should cover if you talk with the people who would be affected by the proposed system. You can learn, for example, what they would want the system to accomplish or what their questions about it might be.

Generating Ideas

Once you have gathered the information you need, you're ready to begin the next phase of the writing process—deciding exactly what to say.

If you have not already written your statement of purpose, now is the time to do so. Try to break the purpose up into several subtopics. For example, suppose the purpose of a client letter is to recommend that the client expand her computerized accounting system. The statement of purpose for this letter could specify the different accounting jobs for which the expanded system would be useful or outline the major advantages of the system.

Another useful technique for generating ideas is brainstorming. With this technique, you think about your topic and write down all the ideas that come to you, in whatever order they come. You don't worry about organizing the ideas, nor do you evaluate them. Just write them down. Later you can consider how, and if, these ideas fit into the outline you developed when you analyzed the document's purposes.

You may find brainstorming easier to do at the computer using a word processor. As you type in the key words and phrases that occur to you, it's possible that the phrases will start to become sentences and the sentences will flow together to become paragraphs. Most people can type faster than they can write with a pencil or pen. You may find that the faster you record your ideas, the more freely the ideas flow. Thus a word processor can be a valuable tool for generating ideas.

Some writers also find that computerized outlining programs help them generate ideas at the computer. These programs can help you organize your thoughts into a structure; they put details into the proper places at the same time they give you a bird's-eye view of the paper's overall organization.

Arranging Your Ideas:
Organization

Once you've decided what you want to say in your paper, it's important to consider how best to arrange these ideas so that the readers will find them easy to follow. In other words, it's time to think about how the document will be organized.

Much of the work you've already done will help you decide on the best pattern of organization. If you've used an outlining program to generate ideas for your paper, for example, the outline you've produced may provide the structure you need for organizing your paper. Keep in mind, though, that you may need to rearrange the sections of the outline so that they will be presented in the most effective order.

Even if you haven't yet arranged your ideas in the form of an outline, other work you've done as part of the preparation of your paper may help you decide on an effective organization. For example, you may be able to use your statement of purpose as the basis of your organization, or your paper may be structured so that the reader's major concerns will be your principle of organization—that is, each concern might be a major division of your paper. Yet another possibility for some documents will be to organize them according to the accounting issues you will address.

When considering all these approaches to organization, and possibly deciding among them, remember this principle: How you organize your documents should be determined by the needs and interests of your readers. Arrange your ideas in the order that they will find most helpful and easiest to follow.

There are a few other principles of organization you should consider as well.

First, nearly all writing has the same basic structure:

Introduction: identifies the subject of the document and tells why it was written. Sometimes the introduction also provides background information about the topic or stresses its importance.

Concise statement of the main ideas: summarizes explicitly your main ideas, conclusions, or recommendations. This part of a document may be part of the introduction or a separate section. It can be as short as a one-sentence statement of purpose or as long as a three-page executive summary in a report.

Development of the main ideas: includes explanations, examples, analyses, steps, reasons, proofs. This part of an outline or paper is often called the body.

Conclusion: brings the paper to an effective close. The conclusion may restate the main idea in a fresh way, suggest further work, or summarize recommendations. An effective conclusion will avoid unnecessary repetition, however.

Later chapters of this handbook will discuss more fully this basic structure as it is used for particular kinds of writing.

Another principle of effective organization is to arrange the ideas in a logical order. For instance, if you were describing the process of reconciling bank statements, you would discuss each step of the procedure in the order in which it is performed.

Finally, you can often organize ideas according to their importance. In business writing, always arrange your ideas from the most to the least important. Note that this principle means you start with the ideas that are most important *to the reader.*

Remember, business documents are not like detective stories. You don't save the best for the last, nor do you keep your readers in suspense about your conclusions.

Suppose you are writing a report to recommend that your firm purchase a new computer system for its accounting records. Naturally, you will want to emphasize the advantages of this purchase—describing them in the order that is likely to be most convincing *to the readers* of the report. However, an investment in a computerized accounting system might also have drawbacks—for example, the cost to purchase and install the equipment and the problems involved in converting to the new system. For your report to appear well researched and unbiased, you will need to include these disadvantages in your discussion. To organize your report, you might use the following basic structure:

I.   Introduction, including your recommendation
II. Body
   A. Advantages, beginning with those most appealing to the readers
   B. Disadvantages, including, when possible, ways to minimize or overcome any drawbacks
III. Conclusion

One final word about organization. Once you've decided how to arrange your ideas, it's a good idea to actually write an outline, if you haven't already done so. Having an outline before you as you draft your paper will help you keep the paper on track as you write; you'll be sure to include all the information you had planned and avoid getting off the subject.

The list of rules for effective writing can now be expanded:

1. **Analyze the purpose of the writing and the needs and expectations of the readers.**
2. **Organize your ideas so that your readers will find them easy to follow.**

WRITING THE DRAFT

The next major step in the writing process is writing the draft. The purpose of this step is to get the ideas down on paper in whatever form they come most easily. Spelling, punctuation, and style are not important in the draft. What is important is to write the ideas down so that later you can polish and correct them.

If you did your brainstorming at the computer, you may already have parts of your draft. This will be the case if the list of ideas you began with evolved into sentences or paragraphs as you typed.

If you have not already begun to work at a word processor, the draft stage of the writing process is an excellent place to start. As we've already pointed out, most people find that they can type at a keyboard faster than they can write with a pencil or pen. Composing your draft at a word processor may thus be faster than composing by hand. It may also be easier, since your ideas will flow more quickly. Your creative stream of thought won't be impeded by the mechanics of writing.

Whether you draft your document at the computer or write it out by hand, the outline you've prepared will guide you as you write. However, you may decide to change the outline as you go, omitting some parts that no longer seem to fit, or adding other ideas that now seem necessary. Changing the outline is fine, because when you revise the draft later you can make sure your thoughts are still well organized.

While you will use your outline as a guide to the ideas you want to include in your draft, you may find it easier to write the various parts of the document in a different order from the one in the outline. Some people find introductions hard to write, so they leave them until last. You may also choose to write the easiest sections of your draft first, or you may start writing some parts of the draft while you are still getting the material together for other parts. If you're composing at a computer, rearranging the parts of your paper is particularly easy, since most word processing programs have commands that enable you to move blocks of text.

One final word of advice on the draft stage: don't allow yourself to get stuck while you search for the perfect word, phrase, or sentence. Leave a blank space or write something that is more-or-less what you mean. You will probably be able to find the right words later when you revise the draft.

REVISING THE DRAFT

The next stage in the writing process is the revision of the draft. It's in this step that you check your grammar and polish your style. Make a final check also to see that the ideas are effectively and completely presented. As you revise your draft, read the document from your reader's point of view.

You will need to revise most of your writing more than once—perhaps even three or four times. The key to revising is to let the writing get cold between revisions; a time lapse between readings will enable you to read more objectively what you have written—what you have actually said, instead of what you meant to say. Ideally, revisions should be at least a day apart.

Another technique that can help you with revision is to have a colleague review your draft for both the content and the effectiveness of the writing. Choose a reviewer that you know is a good writer, and then evaluate the reviewer's suggestions with an open mind.

If you've put your draft on a word processor, you may want to check the text with an editing program or grammar checker. These programs can help you identify certain errors in style, like the sentences that are too long or paragraphs that use the same word too often. Programs are also available that will help you catch some mistakes in punctuation and grammar as well as misspelled words.

A word of caution is in order, though, about these style analyzers and grammar checkers: they're not infallible. They won't catch all the weaknesses in your text, and sometimes they'll flag problems that aren't really there. If you use these programs to analyze your writing, you still have to use your own best judgment about what changes to make.

Another revision technique that works with a word-processed text is to print the document and edit the hard copy by hand. Then you can make the revisions on your disk the next time you work at the computer. Some writers find that they revise more effectively if they work with a hard copy rather than text on a screen.

In sum, if you've put your draft on a word processor, the revision will be much easier and quicker to do than if you have to revise by hand and then retype the entire manuscript. With a few commands to the computer, you can add, delete, or rearrange text. You can insert sentences, change your wording, and move paragraphs around. You can make minor or major changes to your draft, all the time preserving the remainder of your draft without retyping.

The next four chapters of the handbook will discuss what to look for when putting your writing in final form.

We now have three rules for effective writing.

1. **Analyze the purpose of the writing and the needs and expectations of the readers.**
2. **Organize your ideas so that your readers will find them easy to follow.**
3. **Write the draft, and then revise it to make the writing polished and correct.**

THE FINAL DRAFT

After you have polished the style and organization of the paper, you will be ready to put it in its final form. You'll consider questions of document design, such as the use of headings, white space, and other elements of the paper's appearance.

Proofreading is also an important step when you put your paper in its final form. Here are some suggestions for effective proofreading:

1. Proofreading will usually be easier if you leave some time between typing and looking for errors. You will see the paper more clearly if you have been away from it for awhile.
2. If you've drafted your paper on a word processor, use a spelling check program to eliminate spelling and typographical errors. Remember, though, that a computer may not distinguish between homonyms, like *their* and *there,* or *affect* and *effect.*
3. If you don't have access to a word processor, use a dictionary to look up any word that could possibly be misspelled. If you are a poor speller, you might have someone else read your paper for spelling errors.
4. If you know you have a tendency to make a certain type of error, read through your paper at least once to check for that error. For example, if you have problems with verb agreement, check every sentence in your paper to be sure the verbs are correct.
5. Read your paper backwards, sentence by sentence, as a final proofreading step. This technique will isolate each sentence and should make it easier to spot errors you may have overlooked in previous readings.

DEALING WITH WRITER'S BLOCK

Writer's block is a problem all of us face at one time or another. This problem occurs when we stare at blank paper or at a blank screen with no idea of how to get started on the writing task. The ideas and the words just don't come.

Many of the techniques already discussed in this chapter will help you overcome writer's block. In the first place, thinking of writing as a process, rather than a completed product that appears suddenly in its final form, should help make the job less formidable. Any difficult task seems easier if you break it down into manageable steps.

The discussions of the steps in the writing process, especially the section on writing the draft, have included suggestions that will help you overcome writer's block. Here is a summary of these techniques:

1. Plan before you write, so that you know what you need to say.
2. Write with an outline in view, but write the paper in any order you wish. You can rearrange it later.
3. Don't strive for perfection in the draft stage. Leave problems of grammar, spelling, style, and so forth for the revision stage.
4. Begin with the easiest sections to write.
5. Don't get stuck on difficult places. Skip over them and go on to something else. You may find that when you come back to the rough spots later they will not be as hard to write as you had thought at first.

WRITING UNDER PRESSURE

Throughout this chapter, we've seen how writing is easier if you break the project down into steps. It's probably obvious how you can manage these steps when you have plenty of time to work on a paper—lots of time to plan, research, draft, revise, and polish.

But what about those situations where you don't have the luxury of time? What about writing essay questions on an exam, or on-the-job writing tasks where you have only a little while to produce a letter or memo?

The truth is that any writing project, no matter how hurriedly it must be done, will go more smoothly if you stick with the three basic steps of the writing process: plan, draft, and revise. Even if you have only a few minutes to work on a document, allow yourself some of that time to think about who you're writing to, what you need to say, and the best way to organize that material. Then draft the paper.

Allow yourself some time to revise as well. If you have access to a word processor, revision will be much quicker and easier to do. Using a spell check program, which will take only a few minutes for a short memo or letter, can help eliminate embarrassing spelling and typographical errors.

WRITING AT THE COMPUTER

This chapter has frequently discussed ways a computer, especially a word processor, can help you with the writing process. We've mentioned outlining programs and spell checkers, for example; there are also other types of computerized writing aids that you may want to investigate if you have the opportunity. Some writers find these supplementary programs helpful; other writers find that a good word processor with a spelling check program is the only computer help they need.

But what if you don't have ready access to a computer? Of course people wrote well for centuries before computers were ever invented. If you must compose with pencil and paper, you can still write effectively, especially if you follow the steps of the writing process we've been discussing. But writing by hand will take you longer, especially when you revise and polish your draft.

With the widespread availability of computers, both on college campuses and in the workplace, most people can use word processors most of the time for their writing.

It is beyond the scope of this book to discuss particular word processing programs or other computerized aids to writing. But whether you're still in school or already on the job, find out what computer programs are available to you, and learn the features of the programs that will help you to write well. Time spent learning these programs will pay off in papers you can write more effectively, and in less time.

EXERCISES

Exercise 2-1

Among your business correspondents are the following people:

1. The controller of a large corporation—a fellow accountant.
2. A manager in a large corporation—educated and experienced in business, though not an accountant.
3. The owner/president of a medium-sized business (2,500 employees)—experienced in business, but with little formal education.
4. The owner/president of a small business—little business education or experience.
5. Stockholders of a large corporation.
6. A bookkeeper under your supervision.

For each correspondent, which of the following terms or procedures would you *likely* need to explain?

a. GAAP
b. FASB
c. L I F O
d. historical cost
e. lower of cost or market
f. the latest IRS regulations governing depreciation
g. owners' equity
h. quick ratio

i. accounts receivable
j. rent expense
k. double-entry bookkeeping
l. capital leases—accounting for lessee

Exercise 2–2

The society of CPAs in your state is offering a continuing professional education seminar entitled "Effective Writing." You want your firm to give you released time to attend the seminar and you would like to have your expenses paid. Your supervisor, Carol Black, is unfamiliar with the seminar; you will need to convince her that your attendance would benefit the firm by making you a more effective employee. Write a memo to Ms. Black explaining your request.[1]

1. What ideas and information should you include in the memo?
2. How could you arrange this information in an effective order? Write an outline; be careful to include all relevant details about the seminar and an adequate justification for your request.
3. Write the memo. Study Chapter 8 for suggestions on memo organization and format.

Exercise 2–3

What computer equipment and software packages are available on your campus? How can you use these tools to help you with your writing?

Write a memo to your classmates to tell them what computers and programs are available. Consider what information your classmates need and what questions they may ask. For example, if you describe computer labs on campus, your readers will want to know the hours of the lab, the number and types of computers and software packages available, and whether lab assistants are available for help. If you're describing a word processing or editing package, your readers may want to know how these programs can make their writing easier and more effective.

Chapter 8 provides advice on how to write a memo.

NOTES

1. Gadis J. Dillon, "Writing Assignment for Intermediate Accounting" (unpublished class assignment, University of Georgia, 1982).

3

THE FLOW OF THOUGHT
Organizing for Coherence

Chapter 1 identified coherence as one of the three most important qualities of business writing. Coherent writing is organized so that important ideas stand out; the flow of thought is logical and easy to follow.

Chapter 2 introduced some techniques for achieving coherence: analyzing your purpose and the reader's needs, and then planning and outlining before you begin to write. This chapter will discuss additional ways to make your writing coherent. It will explore how to write with unity, use summary sentences and transitions, and structure effective paragraphs and essays.

WRITING WITH UNITY

The key to unified writing is to establish the main idea of each document. An office memo may contain only one paragraph, but that paragraph will have a central idea. A report may run to many pages, but it will still have a central idea or purpose, and probably secondary purposes as well. It's important to decide on your main ideas before you begin writing, preferably before you begin your outline. Deciding on the main idea of a document is similar to analyzing its purpose, as discussed in Chapter 2.

You should be able to summarize a main idea in one sentence. In a paragraph, this sentence is called the topic sentence. In longer documents involving more than two or three paragraphs, this sentence may be called the thesis statement or a statement of purpose.

The main idea is the key to the entire writing task. Every other sentence should be related to it, either directly or indirectly. The central idea is like the hub of a wheel or the trunk of a tree. All other ideas branch off from the central idea; they explain it, analyze it, illustrate it, or prove it. Any sentences or details that are unrelated to the main idea, either directly or indirectly, are irrelevant (off the subject) and should be omitted. In longer documents, entire paragraphs may be irrelevant to the main purpose; these irrelevant paragraphs are called digressions.

When you remove digressions and irrelevant sentences, you achieve unified writing: every sentence, either directly or indirectly, is related to the main idea.

The paragraph below is not unified. Which sentences do you think are irrelevant to the topic sentence?

> (1) Incorporation offers many advantages for a business and its owners. (2) For example, the owners are not responsible for the business's debts. (3) Investors hope to make money when they buy stock in a corporation. (4) Incorporation also enables a business to obtain professional management skills. (5) Corporations are subject to more government regulation than are other forms of organization.

Sentence 1, the topic sentence, identifies what should be the main idea of the paragraph: the advantages of incorporation. Sentences 3 and 5 are off the subject.

Writing with unity is an important way to make your writing coherent.

USING SUMMARY
SENTENCES

Another characteristic of coherent writing is that the main ideas stand out. You can emphasize your main ideas by placing them in the document where they will get the reader's attention.

First, as Chapter 2 suggested, it's important to summarize all of your main ideas at the beginning of your document. For a long document, especially a report, you will need a separate summary section at or near the beginning of the paper. This formal summary may be called an abstract, executive summary, or simply the summary.

When writing these summary sections, be specific and remember your reader's interests and needs. Let's say you are writing a memo to the president of Monroe Sales Company to explain the advantages of using special journals. Summarize those advantages specifically, and relate them to Monroe Sales Company. For example, one of the advantages might be "Special journals save our accounting staff time when we post totals to the ledger."

The summary at the beginning of a document may be several sentences or even pages long, depending on the length of the document and the complexity of your main ideas or recommendations. Here is an example:

> ABC Company should establish the following procedures to ensure a smooth transition to its new computerized system:
> - Management should designate a representative from each department to attend the three-week workshop at company headquarters.
> - Each department should plan a training session for its employees to emphasize the department's use of the system.
> - A two-month transition period should be allowed for converting from the old system.
> - EDP trouble-shooters should be available to all departments to solve any problems that occur.

Summary sentences are important in other places besides the beginning of a document. They are also important to begin each section of the paper and as part of the conclusion.

Any paper that is longer than three or four paragraphs probably has more than one main idea and/or recommendation; each of these ideas is, of course, stated in the introduction or in a separate summary section. Often the logical way to organize the remainder of the document is to use a separate section of the paper to discuss each idea further. Each section will then begin with a summary statement to identify the main idea, or the topic, of that section. The reader will then have a clear idea of what that section is about. It's a good idea, of course, to use somewhat different wording from that used in the beginning of the paper.

The principle we've been discussing sounds simple: Begin with your conclusions, and then give your support. But many writers find it difficult to put into practice. The difficulty may occur because this order of ideas is the reverse of the process writers go through to reach their conclusions. The typical research process is to gather information first and then to arrive at the conclusions. A writer may then try to take the reader through the same investigative steps as those the writer used to solve the problem or answer the question.

Think, though, about your readers' needs. They're mainly interested in the findings of your research, not in the process you went through to get there. They may very well want to read about the facts you considered as well as your analytical reasoning; some readers, in fact, will carefully evaluate the soundness of your data. Their first concern, however, is with the conclusions themselves.

When a paper is organized in the way recommended here, we say that it has a deductive structure: it begins with the conclusions, and then gives the proofs. The opposite of deductive organization is an inductive structure, which gives the data and then presents the conclusions. Research is usually done inductively, but most readers prefer that the results be presented in a deductive organization.

Conclusions may be presented again in a concluding section, especially if the document is very long. Once again, you may need to remind the reader of your main ideas. However, be careful not to sound repetitive; the length and complexity of your document will determine how much detail to include in your conclusion.

TRANSITIONS

Transitions, which are another element of coherent writing, link ideas together. They can be used between sentences, paragraphs, and major divisions of the document. Their purpose is to show the relationship between two ideas: how the second idea flows logically from the first, and how both are related to the main idea of the entire document.

As an example of how transitions work, consider this paragraph. The topic sentence (main idea) is the first sentence; the transitional expressions are in italics:

> (1) Financial statements are important to a variety of users. (2) *First,* investors and potential investors use the statements to decide if a company is a good investment risk. (3) These users look at such factors as net income, the debt-to-equity ratio, and retained earnings. (4) *Second,* creditors use financial statements to decide if a firm is a good credit risk. (5) Creditors want to know if a firm has a large enough cash flow to pay its debts. (6) *Third,* governmental agencies analyze financial statements for a variety of purposes. (7)The Internal Revenue Service, *for example,* will want to know if the company has paid the required amount of taxes on its income. (8) These examples of financial statement users show how diverse their interests can be.

The sentences beginning *first* (2), *second* (4), and *third* (6) give three examples of the paragraph's main idea: the variety of financial statement users. These three sentences relate to one another in a logical, sequential way, which the transitions make clear. These sentences also relate directly to the topic sentence; they illustrate it with specific examples. Sentence 7, which includes the transition *for example,* relates only indirectly to the main idea of the paragraph, but it relates directly to sentence 6. Sentence 7 expresses one example of the purposes financial statements have for government agencies.

Transitions can express a number of relationships between ideas. In the above paragraph, the transitions indicate an enumerated list (2, 4, and 6) and a specific illustration of a general statement (7). Transitions can also imply other relationships between ideas—conclusions, additional information, or contrasts, for example.

To illustrate further the importance of transitions within a paragraph, look at the following example, which lacks transitions:

> Incorporation offers several advantages to businesses and their owners. Ownership is easy to transfer. The business is able to maintain a continuous existence even when the original owners are no longer involved. The stockholders of a corporation are not held responsible for the business's debts. If the XYZ Corporation defaults on a $1 million loan, its investors will not be held responsible for paying that liability. Incorporation enables a business to obtain professional managers with centralized authority and responsibility. The business can be run more efficiently. Incorporation gives a business certain legal rights. It can enter into contracts, own property, and borrow money.

Now see how much easier it is to read the paragraph when it has appropriate transitions:

Incorporation offers several advantages to businesses and their owners. *For one thing,* ownership is easy to transfer, and the business is able to maintain a continuous existence even when the original owners are no longer involved. *In addition,* the stockholders of a corporation are not held responsible for the business's bad debts. If the XYZ Corporation defaults on a $1 million loan, *for example,* its investors will not be held responsible for paying that liability. Incorporation *also* enables a business to obtain professional managers with centralized authority and responsibility; *therefore,* the business can be run more efficiently. *Finally,* incorporation gives a business certain legal rights. *For example,* it can enter into contracts, own property, and borrow money.

Transitional Words and Phrases

Here is a list of frequently used transitional expressions, their meanings, and example sentences showing how some of them work.

Adding a point or piece of information:
and, also, in addition, moreover, furthermore, first/second/third, finally

Accounting is a demanding profession. It can also be financially rewarding.

Making an exception or contrasting point:
but, however, nevertheless, on the other hand, yet, still, on the contrary, in spite of..., nonetheless

The use of historical cost accounting has many drawbacks. Nevertheless, it is still the basis of most accounting procedures.

Giving specific examples or illustrations:
for example, for instance, as an illustration, in particular, to illustrate

Financial statements serve a variety of users. For example, investors use them to evaluate potential investments. Other users include...

Clarifying a point:
that is, in other words, in effect, put simply, stated briefly

The basic accounting equation is *assets equal liabilities plus owners' equity.* That is, $A = L + OE$.

Conceding a point to the opposite side:
granted that, it may be true that, even though, although

Although generally accepted accounting principles are not perfect, their use may offer considerable assurance that financial statements are presented fairly.

Indicating place, time, or importance:
Place: above, beside, beyond, to the right, below, around
Time: formerly, hitherto, earlier, in the past, before, at present, now, today, these days, tomorrow, in the future, next, later on, later
Importance: foremost, most importantly, especially, of less importance, of least importance

In earlier centuries there was no need for elaborate accounting systems. But the size and complexities of today's businesses make modern accounting a complicated process indeed.

Indicating the stages in an argument or process, or the items in a series:
initially, at the outset, to begin with, first, first of all, up to now, so far, second, thus far, next, after, finally, last

The accounting process works in stages. First, transactions must be analyzed.

Giving a result:

as a result, consequently, accordingly, as a consequence, therefore, thus, hence, then, for that reason

Generally accepted accounting principles allow flexibility in their application. Therefore, accountants are able to meet the changing needs of the business world.

Summing up or restating the central point:

In sum, to sum up, to summarize, in summary, to conclude, in brief, in short, as one can see, in conclusion

In conclusion, transitions often make writing much easier to read.

Repetition of Key Words and Phrases

You can use transitional expressions not only between sentences, but also between paragraphs and between major divisions of the document. However, to create continuity between these larger units, you may also use an additional technique—repetition of key words or phrases. The typical location of these repetitions is at the beginning of a new paragraph or section.

The following outline of a student's paper shows the structure of a discussion on alternatives to historical cost accounting. Notice how the combination of transitional expressions and repeated key phrases holds the parts of the report together. These techniques also tie the parts of the report to the main idea of the paper, which is summarized in the thesis statement. Notice also how summary sentences appear throughout the outline.

The Monetary Unit Assumption[1]

I. Introductory paragraph
    A. Attention-getting sentences
        One of the basic assumptions accountants made in the past was that money was an effective common denominator by which business enterprises could be measured and analyzed. Implicit in this assumption was the acceptance of the stable and unchanging nature of monetary units. Recently, however, the validity of this assumption has been questioned not only by academicians and theorists, but by practitioners as well.
    B. Thesis statement (main idea of entire paper)
        Several solutions have been proposed by accountants to correct for the changing value of the monetary unit.
II. Body
    A. Nature of the problem
        The unadjusted monetary unit system has been criticized because it distorts financial statements during periods of inflation.
    B. First solution to the problem
        1. One solution to overstating profits solely because of inflation is to adjust figures for changes in the general purchasing power of the

monetary unit. (This paragraph describes the solution and its advantages.)
   2. However, the general purchasing power approach has been criticized for several reasons. (The paragraph describes the disadvantages of this approach.)
C. Second solution to the problem
   1. Instead of the general purchasing power procedure, some favor adjusting for changes in replacement cost. (Paragraph describes this solution.)
   2. One of the major advantages of the replacement cost approach... (Paragraph discusses several advantages.)
   3. One authority has summarized the criticisms of replacement cost accounting: "Most of the criticisms...." (Paragraph discusses the disadvantages of this approach.)
III. Concluding paragraph
Adjusting for changes in the general purchasing power and adjusting for changes in replacement cost represent attempts to correct the problems of the stable monetary unit assumption in times of inflation.

Pronouns Used to Achieve Coherence

Another tool you can use to achieve coherent writing is the pronoun. A pronoun stands for a noun or a noun phrase that has previously been identified. The noun that the pronoun refers to is called its *antecedent*. Consider this sentence:

Firms usually issue their financial statements at least once a year.

In this sentence, the pronoun *their* refers to the noun *firms*. Put another way, *firms* is the antecedent of *their*.

Because pronouns refer to nouns that the writer has already used, pronouns help connect the thoughts of a paragraph. Look at how the pronouns work in this paragraph:

The audit staff reviewed the financial statements of Tristram Industries to determine if the statements had been prepared in accordance with generally accepted accounting principles. *We* found two problems that may require *us* to issue a qualified opinion. First, Tristram has not been consistent in *its* treatment of contingencies. Second, *we* identified several transactions that may violate the concept of substance over form. *We* suggest a meeting with Tristram's management to discuss these issues.

Pronouns require a word of warning, however. Unless a writer is careful, the reader may not be sure what noun the pronoun refers to. Look at the problem in this sentence:

The managers told the accountants that they did not understand company policy.

Who didn't understand company policy—the managers or the accountants?

This sentence illustrates the problem of ambiguous pronoun reference. Chapter 5 discusses this problem further.

Problems with Transitions

Two problems can occur with the use of transitions, other than the failure to use them when they are needed. The first problem occurs when a writer uses transitional expressions too often. These expressions are necessary to make the relationship of ideas clear when there might be some confusion. Frequently, however, this logical relationship is clear without the use of transitional expressions. Consider this paragraph:

> Accountants never finish their education. They work hard for their college degrees, but after college they must continue studying to stay current on the latest developments in the profession. They must be thoroughly familiar with changing governmental regulations and new pronouncements by professional organizations like the FASB. To improve their professional competence, they participate in a variety of continuing education programs sponsored by such organizations as the AICPA and state accounting societies. Indeed, well-qualified accountants will be lifetime students, always seeking better ways to serve their clients and the public.

Notice how easy this paragraph is to follow, even though it doesn't use a single transitional expression.

The second problem that can occur with transitions is to use the wrong expression, so that an illogical connection of ideas is suggested. Consider these examples:

FAULTY TRANSITION: GAAP are not established by federal law. For instance, organizations such as the FASB issue these standards, and the FASB is not part of the federal government.

REVISED: GAAP are not established by federal law. Rather, organizations that are not part of the federal government, such as the FASB, issue these standards.

FAULTY TRANSITION: If accountants do not follow GAAP, they may lose their CPA licenses. Therefore, they must follow GAAP to conform to their code of professional ethics.

REVISED: If accountants do not follow GAAP, they may lose their CPA licenses. They must also follow GAAP to conform to their code of professional ethics.

Transitions, when used correctly, are a valuable tool for clarifying the relationship between the ideas expressed in your papers. If you use transitions carefully, along with summary sentences and a logical organization, your writing will be easy for your readers to follow.

The next sections of this chapter will show how you can use these techniques to write coherent paragraphs, discussion questions, essays, and other longer forms of writing.

PARAGRAPHS

This section of the chapter will be devoted to techniques of paragraphing: how to plan length, structure, and development so that your paragraphs contribute to coherent writing.

Length

You may not be sure how long paragraphs should be. Are one-sentence paragraphs acceptable? What about paragraphs that run on for nearly an entire typed page?

One rule is that a paragraph should be limited to the development of one idea. Thus, the length of most paragraphs is somewhere between one sentence and an entire page. However, an occasional short paragraph, even of only one sentence, may be effective to emphasize an idea or to provide a transition between two major divisions of the writing.

You should be wary, however, of long paragraphs, which look intimidating and are often hard to follow. You may need to divide a long paragraph into two or more shorter ones. Appropriate transitions can tie the new paragraphs together and maintain a smooth flow of thought.

A good rule of thumb is to limit most of your paragraphs to four or five sentences.

Structure

Another feature of well-written paragraphs is their structure. We have already suggested that a strong topic sentence can contribute to a unified, coherent paragraph. A topic sentence states the main idea of the paragraph. It is usually the first sentence in the paragraph, and sometimes it contains a transition tying the new paragraph to the previous one. All other sentences in the paragraph should develop the idea expressed in the topic sentence.

Two patterns of paragraph organization are useful for accountants' writing tasks—the simple-deductive paragraph and the complex-deductive paragraph. The simple-deductive arrangement states the main idea in the first sentence (topic sentence); all other sentences *directly* develop that idea through explanation, illustration, or analysis. A concluding sentence is sometimes helpful. Look again at this paragraph, which illustrates a simple-deductive organization.

> (1) Accountants never finish their education. (2) They work hard for their college degrees, but after college they must continue studying to stay current on the latest developments in the profession. (3) They must be thoroughly familiar with changing governmental regulations and new pronouncements by professional organizations like the FASB. (4) To improve their professional competence, they participate in a variety of continuing education programs sponsored by such organizations as the AICPA and state accounting societies. (5) Indeed, well-qualified accountants will be lifetime students, always seeking better ways to serve their clients and the public.

In this paragraph, sentence 1 is the topic sentence, sentences 2–4 develop the main idea, and sentence 5 is the conclusion. A simple-deductive paragraph has a simple structural diagram such as this one:

    (1)   Topic sentence—main idea
        (2)   Supporting sentence
        (3)   Supporting sentence
        (4)   Supporting sentence
    (5)   Concluding sentence (optional)

A complex-deductive paragraph has a more elaborate structure. This paragraph is complex deductive:

> (1) Financial statements are important to a variety of users. (2) First, investors and potential investors use the statements to decide if a company is a good investment risk. (3) These users look at such factors as net income, the debt-to-equity ratio, and retained earnings. (4) Second, creditors use financial statements to decide if a firm is a good credit risk. (5) Creditors want to know if a firm has a large enough cash flow to pay its debts. (6) Third, governmental agencies analyze financial statements for a variety of purposes. (7) The Internal Revenue Service, for example, will want to know if the company has paid the required amount of taxes on its income. (8) These examples of financial statement users show how diverse their interests can be.

In this paragraph, sentence 1 (the topic sentence) states the main idea. Sentence 2 directly supports the main idea by giving an example of it, but sentence 3 explains sentence 2. Thus sentence 3 directly supports sentence 2, but only indirectly supports sentence 1. Complex-deductive paragraphs have a structural diagram similar to this one:

    (1)   Topic sentence—main idea
        (2)   Direct support
            (3)   Indirect support
        (4)   Direct support
            (5)   Indirect support
        (6)   Direct support
            (7)   Indirect support
    (8)   Conclusion (optional)

Complex-deductive paragraphs can have numerous variations. The number of direct supporting sentences can vary, as can the number of indirect supports. Sometimes direct supports may not require any indirect supports.

Consider another example of a complex-deductive paragraph:

> (1) Two of the most popular inventory flow assumptions used by businesses today are FIFO (first-in, first-out) and LIFO (last-in, first-out). (2) FIFO assumes that the first goods purchased for inventory are the first goods sold. (3) Therefore, ending inventory under FIFO consists of the most recent purchases. (4) Because older, usually lower costs are matched with sales revenues, FIFO results in a higher net

income and thus higher income tax liabilities. (5) The LIFO flow assumption, on the other hand, assumes that the most recent purchases are the first goods sold. (6) Cost of goods sold, however, will be based on more recent, higher prices. (8) Thus LIFO usually results in lower net income and lower income tax liabilities. (9) This advantage makes LIFO very popular with many businesses.

This paragraph can be outlined to reveal the following structure:

1.   Topic sentence (1): Two popular inventory flow assumptions
     A.   FIFO (2–4)
          1.   Description (2)
          2.   Effect on inventory (3)
          3.   Effect on net income and taxes (4)
     B.   LIFO (5–9)
          1.   Description (5)
          2.   Effect on inventory (6)
          3.   Effect on net income and taxes (7–8)
          4.   Popularity (9)

The descriptions of FIFO and LIFO in this paragraph are, of course, very condensed—probably too condensed for most purposes. Moreover, the paragraph is really too long. It would be better to divide it between sentences four and five. The result would be two shorter, but closely related paragraphs. Both would have simple-deductive structures. However, the first paragraph would be a modified version of a simple-deductive structure, because the main idea of this paragraph would be the second sentence.

The important idea about both simple- and complex-deductive paragraphs is their unity; all sentences, either directly or indirectly, develop the main idea of the paragraph as expressed in the topic sentence.

Some writers may wonder about a third type of paragraph organization— paragraphs with an inductive structure. Inductive paragraphs put the main idea last; supporting sentences lead up to the topic sentence, which is, of course, the last sentence in the paragraph.

For most business writing, inductive paragraphs are not as effective as simple- or complex-deductive paragraphs. Business readers like to identify main ideas from the start; they don't like to be kept in suspense, wondering "What's all this leading up to? What's the point?" So it's a good idea to stick with deductive organization for most, if not all, of your paragraphs.

Paragraph Development

An effective paragraph is not only well organized; it is also well developed. That is, the idea expressed in the topic sentence is adequately explained and illustrated so that the reader has a clear understanding of what the writer wishes to say.

Several techniques are useful for paragraph development: descriptive and factual details, illustrations or examples, definitions, and appeals to authority.

Descriptive and factual details give a more thorough, concrete explanation of the idea expressed in a general way in the topic sentence. Factual details give measurable, observable, or historical information that can be objectively verified. Descriptive details are similar to factual details: they give specific characteristics of the subject being discussed.

When you use details with which your readers are familiar, they will be better able to understand your observations and conclusions. In the following paragraph, the main idea is stated in the first sentence. The paragraph is then developed with factual details:

> Our net income for this year has declined because we've lost one of our most important customers. Owen Industries, which last year ordered over $4 million in automotive supplies from our Detroit plant, has gone into bankruptcy. The loss of this account has caused our revenues to decline by 15 percent.

Another useful technique of paragraph development is illustrations or examples—typical cases or specific instances of the idea being discussed. Illustrations can take a variety of forms. Sometimes a paragraph will combine several brief examples, or it may use one long, extended illustration. The examples may be factually true, or they may be hypothetical—invented for the purpose of illustration.

Definitions are useful to explain concepts or terms which might be unfamiliar to the reader. A definition can be formal, such as the meaning given in a dictionary or an accounting standard, or it can be a more informal explanation of a term. Frequently a definition is more effective when combined with an illustration.

Here is a paragraph developed by definition and illustration:

> *Assets* can be defined as "economic resources—things of value—owned by a business."[2] For example, cash is an asset; so are the land, buildings, and equipment owned by a business. Sometimes assets are resources legally owned by a business, though not tangible. An example of this kind of asset is an account receivable.

Finally, some paragraphs are developed by appeals to authority—facts, illustrations, or ideas obtained from a reputable source such as a book, article, interview, or official pronouncement. Appeals to authority may be paraphrases—someone else's idea expressed in your own words—or direct quotations from the source being used. The paragraph above uses a direct quotation from an accounting textbook to provide an authoritative definition of *assets*. Chapter 10 gives more information on the correct use of quotations and paraphrases.

By using a variety of techniques, then, you can develop fully the ideas expressed in the topic sentences of your paragraphs. Factual and descriptive detail, illustration, definition, and authority—all of these techniques give the reader a clear understanding of what you wish to explain.

However you decide to develop your paragraphs, remember the importance of your reader's interests and needs. It's better to select supporting details and examples with which the reader is already familiar.

DISCUSSION QUESTIONS
AND ESSAYS

A section about discussion questions and essays might sound too academic for a writing handbook for accountants. However, many accounting students take exams with discussion questions, and essay questions are an important part of the CPA exam. In addition, many of the principles of organizing and developing an essay are applicable to memos, reports, and other types of writing used by accountants in practice.

Discussion Questions

The key to answering a short discussion question (one to three paragraphs) is well-organized paragraphs with strong topic sentences. Usually the question itself will suggest the topic sentence. For example, consider this question:

Discuss who the users of financial statements are.

The answer to this question might begin with the following sentence:

The users of an organization's financial statements are mainly external to the organization.

The first paragraph of the answer would discuss external users—investors, creditors, government agencies, etc. A second, shorter paragraph might then discuss internal users of financial statements, such as management and employees. The second topic sentence might be as follows:

People within an organization are also interested in its financial statements.

Short paragraphs with strong topic sentences will help the exam grader identify your main ideas, and thus give you credit for what you know.

Essays

Before you read this section, review the discussion of paragraph development earlier in this chapter. Pay particular attention to the complex-deductive pattern of organization.

Complex-deductive paragraphs have a main idea (topic sentence) supported by major and minor supports. Essays—discussions of four or more paragraphs—are organized the same way, except that the main idea (thesis statement) has as its major supports paragraphs rather than sentences. In addition, the thesis statement may come at the end of the first paragraph, in which case it will be preceded by attention-getting sentences. Here is the outline of a five-paragraph essay:

   I. Introduction—first paragraph
      A. Attention-getting sentences (optional)
      B. Thesis statement—main idea of the essay, usually expressed in one sentence
  II. Body of the essay—develops the thesis through analysis, explanation, examples, proofs, or steps
      A. Major support—second paragraph
         1.
         2.   minor supports—sentences that develop the paragraph in a simple- or complex-deductive organization
         3. etc.
      B. Major support—third paragraph
         1.
         2.   minor supports
         3.
      C. Major support—fourth paragraph
         1.
         2.   minor supports
         3.
 III. Conclusion—fifth paragraph
      A. Repeats the essay's main idea—a variation of the thesis statement
      B. Forceful ending

Some of the parts of this outline need more discussion.

Attention-getting sentences.   Some essays being with attention-getting sentences, which are used to get the reader interested in the subject. Several techniques can be used:

- Give background information about the topic. Why is the topic of current interest?
- Pose a problem or raise a question (to be answered in the essay).
- Define key terms, perhaps the topic itself.
- Show the relevance of the topic to the reader.
- Begin with an interesting direct quotation.
- Relate a brief anecdote relevant to the topic.
- Relate the specific topic to a wider area of interest.

The following essay introduction uses two of these techniques. It poses a question and then suggests the relevance of the topic to the reader, if we assume that the essay was written for an audience of accountants. The final sentence of the paragraph is the thesis statement.

Do accountants need to be good writers? Some people would answer "No" to this question. They believe an accountant's job is limited to arithmetical calculations with very little need to use words or sentences. But this picture of an accountant's responsibilities is a misconception. In fact, good writing skills are essential to the successful practice of accounting.

Sometimes you may choose not to use attention-getting sentences, but decide instead to begin your essay with the thesis statement. This is a particularly good strategy to use for exam questions.

Thesis statement.   The thesis statement summarizes the main idea of the essay, usually in one sentence. It may be a *simple* thesis statement, such as the one in the paragraph above. Alternatively, the thesis statement may be *expanded*. That is, it may summarize the main supports of the discussion. Here is an example of an expanded thesis statement:

> In fact, successful accountants must have good writing skills to communicate with clients, managers, agencies, and colleagues.

Sometimes, to avoid a long or awkward sentence, you may want to use two sentences for the thesis statement:

> In fact, good writing skills are essential to the successful practice of accounting. For example, during a typical business day an accountant may write to clients, managers, agencies, or colleagues.

Conclusion.   A conclusion will usually do at least one thing: repeat the essay's main idea, usually in some variation of the thesis statement. In addition, conclusions often end with a forceful statement that will stay in the reader's mind, thus giving the discussion a more lasting impact. For a strong ending you can use several techniques, many of which resemble those used in the introduction:

- Show a broad application of the ideas suggested in the discussion.
- End with an authoritative direct quotation that reinforces your position.
- Challenge the reader.
- Echo the attention-getting sentences. For example, if you began by posing a question in the introduction, you can answer it explicitly in the conclusion.

If you're writing an essay on an exam, a concluding paragraph may not be necessary. It's important, though, that the essay seem finished. It will likely seem complete if you've developed your thesis statement fully.

Applying Essay Techniques to Other Kinds of Writing

If you are answering an essay question on an exam, you can use the techniques just discussed to organize and develop an effective discussion. But how do these techniques work with the writing formats more typically used by accountants— letters, memos, and reports?

First of all, everything you write should have a main idea. In an essay this idea is called the thesis statement; in a memo or report the main idea might be included in the statement of purpose. But whatever you're writing, it's a good idea to identify the main idea before you even begin your outline. Unless this idea is clear in your mind—or clearly written in your notes—what you write may be rambling and confusing. Your reader might then wonder, "What's this person trying to say? What's the point?"

So whatever you write should be organized around a central idea, just as an essay is organized. Letters, reports, and memos share other features of an essay as well: a basic three-part structure (introduction, body, conclusion); complex-deductive organization; and the need for adequate transitions and concrete support.

If you understand the principles discussed in this chapter, you will have an easier job planning and organizing the writing tasks which are part of your professional responsibilities.

Sample Essay

Below is an actual assignment for an essay in an intermediate accounting class. Figure 3–1 shows a student's answer that illustrates some of the principles of good organization and development.

Assignment.[3]   A small company has just hired you to replace its bookkeeper, who left for Barbados with a sales manager. Before the bookkeeper resigned, she explained the accounting system to the company president. In his 15-minute review of the system, the president learned his company had a general journal, four special journals, a general ledger, and two subsidiary ledgers.

His first suggestion to you is that you cut costs and reduce duplication of effort. He suggests that you use only one journal instead of five and does not see any need for ledgers since they only duplicate what is already recorded in the journal.

Explain in 300–500 words how the president's suggestions may increase rather than reduce costs, and require more rather than less effort.

This chapter has added four rules to our list of effective writing skills. We now have seven rules:

1. **Analyze the purpose of the writing and the needs and expectations of the readers.**
2. **Arrange your ideas so that your readers will find them easy to follow.**
3. **Write the draft, and then revise it to make the writing polished and correct.**
4. **Make the writing unified—all sentences should relate to the main idea, either directly or indirectly. Eliminate digressions and irrelevant detail.**
5. **Use summary sentences and transitions to make your writing coherent.**
6. **Write in short paragraphs that begin with clear topic sentences.**
7. **Develop paragraphs by illustration, definition, detail, and appeals to authority.**

Why Journals and Ledgers are Important

Good accounting, like good management, relies on an organized system and a division of labor to reduce costs and minimize effort. Multiple journals and ledgers actually save the company time and money by isolating related accounts, delegating details, and summarizing information in controlling accounts. Isolation, delegation, and summarization free the accountant from the time-consuming task of sorting through overcrowded controlling accounts, thereby minimizing effort and reducing cost.

Isolation of accounts into special journals and subsidiary ledgers allows the accountant or manager to collect information on specific accounts in a small amount of time. Special journals, categorized as Cash Receipts, Sales on Account, Purchases on Account, and Payments of Cash, isolate each of these activities. Data can be reviewed for timely managerial decisions at a moment's notice because special journals eliminate the need to sort through other transactions. Likewise, subsidiary ledgers keep a running total of balances in a related category. The information remains separate and easily accessible and therefore of greatest use not only to the accountant, but also to management.

Delegation of transactions into special and subsidiary records eliminates clutter in controlling accounts and also allows for ease of data collection. For example, Herb Company has 2,000 customers and over 50 creditors. The accountant uses subsidiary ledgers to organize these accounts into visible information. If a creditor double-bills the company, a quick check of that

FIGURE 3-1 Example of an Essay[4]

ledger will reveal the problem. Searching through a cluttered
control account for the same information would prove tedious and
leave room for error. Although the use of subsidiary ledgers
does require double posting, the initial expenditure of time more
than repays itself in time and money saved. Those 2,000 customers
and over 50 creditors need room in subsidiary ledgers to free
control accounts for other important transactions.

Finally, summarization of subsidiary and special records
occurs in the controlling accounts, providing the accountant and
management with an overall view of the company's transactions.
Interested parties "get the big picture" without seeing all of
the transactions at once because all account totals are posted
to control accounts.

Cost reduction and labor savings result from the isolation,
delegation, and summarization processes. Although account cutbacks
may seem at first to provide an easy solution, after closer
inspection the true picture emerges. Control accounts, supported
by additional journals and ledgers, actually save time because
of their unique organization, and that saves money.

FIGURE 3-1, con't.

TEST YOURSELF

1. For the following paragraph identify the

    *   Topic sentence
    *   Structure (simple-deductive or complex-deductive)
    *   Major and minor supporting ideas, *if* this is a complex-deductive paragraph
    *   Transitional devices
    *   Techniques of development (factual and/or descriptive detail, single or multiple examples, definition, appeal to authority, or a combination of techniques)

(1) One career alternative for accounting graduates is to work for a government. (2) Government accountants oversee the financial records of federal, state, and local agencies. (3) They also examine the records of individuals and businesses that are subject to government regulations. (4) Employees of the Internal Revenue Service, for example, often examine business records supporting tax returns. (5) Performing services similar to management accountants, government accountants also budget administrative costs and plans for future operations, record transactions and events, prepare financial statements, and electronically process accounting data for government bureaucracies.[5]

2. Is the following paragraph coherent? If not, revise it to improve its organization, using some of these techniques:

    *   A strong topic sentence stating the paragraph's main idea
    *   Transitional devices showing the relation between sentences
    *   Elimination of sentences that don't fit
    *   Division of long, disunified paragraphs into shorter, unified ones
    *   Rearranging sentences by grouping ideas together (add sentences if necessary)

    > Government accountants help national, state, and local governments control spending and budgeting. Government spending could run rampant. Government accounting is similar to industrial accounting in many of its functions. Government accountants help prevent the government from wasting taxpayers' money.

TEST YOURSELF—ANSWERS

1.   *   Topic sentence: (1)
      *   Structure: complex-deductive
      *   Supports
         major: (2), (3), (5)
         minor: (4)
      *   Transitional devices:
         (2) government—repetition of key word

(3) they—pronoun
    also—transitional expression
    government—repetition of key word

(4) for example—transitional expression

(5) government accountants—repetition of key phrase
    also—transitional expression
    government—repetition of key word

* Techniques of development:
  details, examples

2. This paragraph needs revision. Here is one possibility:
   Government accountants help national, state, and local governments control spending and budgeting. Without controls, government spending could run rampant. Thus, one function of government accountants is to help prevent the government from wasting taxpayers' money.

EXERCISES

Exercise 3-1

Peter Dowling is a junior staff accountant for a small CPA firm in Austin, Texas. The senior partners have asked him to investigate two computer systems for possible purchase by the firm. The partners have also asked him to recommend the system that the firm should buy. Peter has drafted the following outline for his report and asked for your critique.

  I. Introduction
 II. The history of computer technology
III. Simple Sam Computer Model B-13
     A. General description of features
     B. Nearest service center in Dallas, Texas
     C. Can handle much of the firm's computer work
     D. Limited capacity for future expansion
     E. Takes up only a small amount of office space
 IV. Whiz Kid Computer Model 1004
     A. Easily adaptable in the future to new programs and functions
     B. Slightly larger than the Simple Sam Model
     C. Service center in Austin
     D. Can handle all the firm's current computer work
     E. General description of features
  V. The need for accountants to have more training in computer science
 VI. The role of computers in the future of accounting
VII. Conclusion

1. What is the purpose of Peter's report?
2. What do you think is the main idea of the report?
3. What material included in Peter's outline is irrelevant to his purpose?
4. What necessary information has he forgotten to include?
5. Are the ideas in the outline arranged logically? If not, rearrange the ideas into a more effective outline. Include only relevant material.

6. What kinds of transitional devices could Peter use when he writes his report? Rewrite the outline in sentence form, and include transitional devices.

Exercise 3-2

For the following paragraphs, identify

- Topic sentence
- Structure (simple-deductive or complex-deductive)
- Major and minor supporting ideas in complex-deductive paragraphs
- Transitional devices
- Techniques of development (factual and/or descriptive detail, single or multiple examples, definition, appeal to authority, or a combination of techniques)

1. (1) The accounting profession may be classified in many ways; a major classification is public accounting and private accounting. (2) "Public" accountants are those whose services are rendered to the general public on a fee basis. (3) Such services include auditing, income taxes, and management consulting. (4) "Private" accountants are all the rest. (5) They consist of not only those individuals who work for businesses, but also those who work for government agencies, including the Internal Revenue Service.[6]

2. (1) An accounting system is a formal means of gathering data to aid and coordinate collective decisions in light of the overall goals or objectives of an organization. (2) The accounting system is the major quantitative information system in almost every organization. (3) An effective accounting system provides information for three broad purposes or ends: internal reporting to managers, for use in planning and controlling routine operations; internal reporting to managers, for use in strategic planning—that is, the making of special decisions and the formulating of overall policies and long-range plans; and external reporting to stockholders, government, and other outside parties.[7]

3. (1) Purchase options on land represent payments to the owners of property giving one the right during a specified period to buy a site or pass up the purchase opportunity. (2) Accounting for these options presents problems for today's accountant. (3) He or she must decide whether to capitalize the cost of the option in a land account or to expense the cost in the immediate period. (4) Further complications exist when clients acquire several options on suitable sites with intentions of choosing the best alternative. (5) Here, the accountant must consider several factors before recording the costs incurred, including materiality and future expectations.[8]

Exercise 3-3

Some of the following paragraphs are effectively organized, but some lack unity and/or coherence. Analyze the paragraphs to decide which ones need revision. Then revise the faulty paragraphs, using some of these techniques:

- A strong topic sentence stating the paragraph's main idea
- Transitional devices showing the relation between sentences
- Elimination of sentences that don't fit
- Divison of long, disunified paragraphs into shorter, unified ones
- Rearranging sentences by grouping relevant ideas together (add sentences if necessary)

1. One service that public accountants perform is auditing. Accountants examine clients' financial statements to see if they are in conformity with generally accepted accounting principles. Accountants give credibility to financial statements. Public accountants offer management consulting services. Management consultants suggest ways firms can improve such functions as information processing, budgeting, and accounting systems. Taxes are an increasingly complex area. Accountants prepare and file returns and advise clients how to incur the smallest tax liability on a transaction.

2. Many corporations can benefit from convertible debt. Firms should be aware of the hardships that may arise from conversion or nonconversion. Firms should be aware that accounting requirements impose a potentially unfavorable effect on earnings per share. Corporations want to obtain low-cost funds now, and desire also to increase their equity in the future.[9]

3. Although the purchase of our supplier's stock may offer us several advantages, there are also some potential problems we should consider. For one thing, we may not always need the supplier's raw material, because we may not always manufacture the product that requires this material. And even if we continue to manufacture our product, our research and development staff may develop a cheaper, synthetic raw material. Finally, if we do purchase the stock but later need to resell it, we cannot be assured that the stock will be marketable at that time.

Exercise 3-4

Discuss the following topics in well-organized and well-developed paragraphs or essays.

1. Conservatism
2. Foreign Corrupt Practices Act
3. Internal control
4. Reversing entries
5. Stockholders' equity
6. Cash
7. Responsibility accounting
8. Capitalization
9. Cost center
10. Direct labor
11. FASB

12. GAAP
13. Tax deferral
14. Double-entry accounting

Exercise 3-5

Discuss the topics defined below, using the techniques covered in this and earlier chapters. Your answers might range from one to five paragraphs or more, depending on the topic.

1. Contrast financial and managerial accounting.
2. Define and discuss depreciation as used in accounting.
3. Discuss why intraperiod tax allocation is necessary.
4. Contrast cash-basis accounting with accrual accounting.
5. Discuss the history of standard-setting bodies for accounting in the United States.

NOTES

1. Steven C. Dabbs, "The Monetary Unit Assumption" (unpublished student paper, University of Georgia, 1978).
2. Jack E. Kiger, Stephen E. Loeb, and Gordon S. May, *Accounting Principles,* 2nd ed. (New York: Random House, 1987), p. 1062.
3. William Timothy O'Keefe, "Writing Assignment for Intermediate Accounting" (unpublished class assignment, University of Georgia, 1980).
4. Sandra L. Herbelin, "Journals and Ledgers" (unpublished student paper, University of Georgia, 1980).
5. Allan Bashinski, "Accounting Careers" (unpublished student paper, University of Georgia, 1982).
6. Adapted from Charles T. Horngren, *Introduction to Financial Accounting,* 3rd ed. (Englewood Cliffs, N.J.: Prentice-Hall, Inc., 1987). p. 5. Reprinted by permission.
7. Charles T. Horngren, *Introduction to Management Accounting,* 7th ed. (Englewood Cliffs, N.J.: Prentice-Hall, Inc., 1987), p. 3. Reprinted by permission.
8. Greg Thompson, "Land Option Costs" (unpublished student paper, University of Georgia, 1982).
9. Jean Bryan, "Finance and Accounting Considerations in Issuing Convertible Debt" (unpublished student paper, University of Georgia, 1980).

4

A SENSE OF STYLE
Writing with Conciseness and Clarity

So far in this book we have looked at writing mainly as an organizational task: planning the structure and contents of the paper so that it achieves its purpose in a way the readers will find meaningful. We have stressed the quality of coherence: writing that is easy to follow, with main ideas that stand out. Previous chapters have looked at writing in terms of large units. They have discussed the structure of the paper as a whole, and the organization of sections and paragraphs.

We turn now to a more detailed level of effective writing. This chapter looks at word choices and sentence structures that contribute to a vigorous, readable writing style. In this discussion of style, we will emphasize two other important qualities of effective writing: conciseness and clarity.

CONCISENESS

Chapter 3 has already suggested several ways to make your writing more concise. The fourth rule of effective writing tells us to eliminate digressions and irrelevant detail. In general, we can define concise writing as that which contains no unnecessary elements—no extra words, phrases, sentences, or paragraphs.

Be concise—make every word count.

Unnecessary Words

The easiest way to be concise (make every word count) is to see how many words you can cross out of your writing, often with only a simple revision of the sentence. Beware of dead words—words that fill up space without adding meaning. Here are some examples of sentences littered (and padded) with dead words:

WORDY: This disclosure has the capacity of providing important information to creditors and investors. (13 words)
CONCISE: This disclosure can provide important information to creditors and investors. (10 words)
WORDY: For the sake of our tax liability reduction goals, we changed the way we accounted for the purchase. (18 words)
CONCISE: To reduce our tax liability, we changed the way we accounted for the purchase. (14 words)
WORDY: There is one organization that has been very influential in improving the profession of accounting—the AICPA. (17 words)
CONCISE: The AICPA has improved the accounting profession significantly. (8 words)
WORDY: We hope the entire staff will assist us in our efforts to reduce costs. (14 words)
CONCISE: We hope the entire staff will help us reduce costs. (10 words)
WORDY: The estimates range all the way from $100 to $350. (10 words)
CONCISE: The estimates range from $100 to $350. (7 words)

Watch out for "there is" and "there are." They can usually be eliminated. "The fact that," "which is," and "which are" can sometimes be left out:

WORDY: I would like to call your attention to the fact that our earnings last month were down fifty percent. (19 words)
CONCISE: Remember that our earnings were down fifty percent last month. (10 words)
                        or (even better)
          Our earnings dropped fifty percent last month. (7 words)
WORDY: In spite of the fact that our costs rose by ten percent, we still were able to keep our prices stable. (21 words)
CONCISE: Although costs rose by ten percent, our prices remained stable. (10 words)
WORDY: His partner, who is an engineer, . . .
CONCISE: His partner, an engineer, . . .

Simplicity

Another way to make your writing concise is to write as simply as possible. Sometimes writers get into the habit of using big words and long, complicated sentences. Such writing is hard to read. Look at the following sentence:

An increase in an employee's rate of pay will not become effective prior to the date on which the employee has completed a minimum of 13 weeks' actual work at his regular occupational classification.

If we simplify this sentence, it will be easier to understand:

An employee must work at least 13 weeks at his regular job before he can receive an increase in pay.[1]

Sometimes words and sentences get so complicated that their meaning is completely lost:

> Ultimate consumer means a person or group of persons, generally constituting a domestic household, who purchase eggs generally at the individual stores of retailers or purchase and receive deliveries of eggs at the place of abode of the individual or domestic household from producers or retail route sellers and who use such eggs for their consumption as food.

Translation:

> Ultimate consumers are people who buy eggs to eat them.[2]

Therefore, another technique for effective writing style is simplicity.

Keep it simple—simple vocabulary and short sentences.

Good writers will use short, everyday words as much as possible. For example, they will usually write *use* instead of *utilize, help* instead of *assistance.* Shorter, familiar words are easier to read and make writing more forceful.

The chart in Table 4-1 shows two columns of words. Column B lists short, familiar words; Column A lists longer, more difficult words that are often substituted for the everyday words in Column B. The table also shows how single words (*because*) can often replace phrases (*for the reason that*). As a general rule, use the words and phrases in Column B rather than those in Column A. Some of the terms in Column A can be omitted entirely (for example, *it should be noted that*).

Another way to achieve a simple, readable style is to use short sentences. Short sentences are particularly important when you are explaining complicated ideas.

The average sentence should be about 15 words long.

Note that 15 words is an *average.* Some sentences will be longer, some shorter. In fact, it's a good idea to vary sentence lengths so the writing doesn't become monotonous. Sentence variation will be discussed again later in this chapter.

TABLE 4-1 Simplifying Word Choices
As a rule, use the words and phrases in Column B rather than those in Column A.

COLUMN A	COLUMN B
above-mentioned firms	these firms
absolutely essential	essential
activate	begin
advise	tell
aggregate	total
along the lines of	like

TABLE 4-1 Simplifying Word Choices (cont.)

COLUMN A	COLUMN B
anticipate	expect
as per your request	as you requested
assist	help
at all times	always
at this point in time	now
at this time	now
attempt	try
commence	begin
communicate	write, tell
completely eliminated	eliminated
comprise	include
consider	think
constitute	are, is
discontinue	stop
disutility	uselessness
due to the fact that	because, since
during the time that	while
earliest convenience	promptly
effort	work
enclosed herewith	enclosed
enclosed please find	enclosed is
endeavor	try
exercise care	be careful
facilitate	ease, simplify
failed to	didn't
few in number	few
for the purpose of	for
for the reason that	since
from the point of view that	for
furnish	send, give
i.e.	that is
implement	carry out
in advance of	before
in all cases	always
inasmuch as	since, because
in behalf of	for
in connection with	about
in many cases	often
in most cases	usually
indicate	show, point out
initiate	begin
in terms of	in
in the amount of	of, for
in the case of	if
in the event that (of)	if
in the nature of	like
in the neighborhood of	about
in this case	here
investigate	study
in view of the fact that	because, since

TABLE 4-1 Simplifying Word Choices (cont.)

COLUMN A	COLUMN B
it has come to my attention	Ms. Jones has just told me; I have just learned
it is felt	I feel; we feel
it is our understanding that	we understand that
it should be noted that	omit
maintain	keep
maintain cost control	control cost
make an analysis	analyze
make a purchase	buy
make application to	apply
make contact with	see, meet
maximum	most, largest
minimum	least, smallest
modification	change
obtain	get
on the order of	about
on the part of	by
optimum	best
past history	history
per annum	annually, per year
period of time	time, period
pertaining to	about, for
philosophy	plan, idea
please be advised that	omit
please don't hesitate to call on us	please write us
prepare an analysis	analyze
presently	now
prior to	before
procure	get, buy
provide	give
provide continuous indication	indicate continuously
pursuant to your inquiry	as you requested
range all the way from	range from
regarding	about
relative to	about
represent	be, is, are
require	need
so as to	to
subsequent to	after, later
substantial	large, big
sufficient	enough
terminate	end, stop
the major part of	most of
the manner in which	how
the undersigned; the writer	I, me
through the use of	by, with
true facts	facts
thereon, thereof, thereto, therefrom	omit
this is to acknowledge	thank you for, I have receiveu
this is to inform you that we shall send	we'll send

TABLE 4-1 Simplifying Word Choices (cont.)

COLUMN A	COLUMN B
transpire	happen
under separate cover	by June 1, tomorrow, separately, by parcel post
until such time as	until
utilize	use
vital	important
with a view to	to
with reference to	about
with regard to	about
with respect to	on, for, of, about
with the object to	to
with the result that	so that

Verbs and Nouns

Another technique to make writing more concise is to use active verbs and descriptive nouns, rather than lots of adverbs and adjectives.

Write with active verbs and descriptive nouns.

See how this sentence can be improved:

WORDY: There are some serious, unfortunate results of accounting based on historical cost during times of decreasing purchasing power of the monetary unit. (22 words)

CONCISE: Historical cost accounting creates problems during periods of inflation. (9 words)

One frequent cause of wordy writing is hidden verbs. For example,

causes a misstatement of
instead of
misstates

provides a matching of
instead of
matches

makes an analysis of
instead of
analyzes

will serve as an explanation of
instead of
will explain

What are the hidden verbs in these sentences?

> We should not make reference to any prior years' financial statements in our report.
>
> The company's history of marginal performance over the past several years may be an indication of future solvency problems.

In the first sentence, the hidden verb is *refer;* in the second sentence, it is *indicate.* The revised sentences are a little less wordy, a little more forceful:

> We should not refer to any prior years' financial statements in our report.
>
> The company's history of marginal performance over the past several years may indicate future solvency problems.

Here are some other sentences with hidden verbs, followed by revisions to make them more concise:

HIDDEN VERB: I will make a recommendation concerning the best way to record this transaction. (13 words)

REVISED: I will recommend the best way to record this transaction. (10 words)

HIDDEN VERB: I have come to the conclusion that we should update our equipment. (12 words)

REVISED: I have concluded that we should update our equipment. (9 words)

HIDDEN VERB: This method will result in a distribution of the costs between the balance sheet and the income statement. (18 words)

REVISED: This method will distribute the costs between the balance sheet and the income statement. (14 words)

HIDDEN VERB: We are able to make the determination of the historical cost of an asset due to the fact that we have records of its purchase. (25 words)

REVISED: We can determine an asset's historical cost because we have records of its purchase. (14 words)

Finally, avoid sentence introductions that weaken the sentence idea. Don't apologize for or hedge about what you're saying:

WORDY: It has come to my attention that our department has overrun its budget for supplies. (15 words)

CONCISE: Our department has overrun its budget for supplies. (8 words)

WORDY: This report is an attempt to explain the proper accounting treatment for loss contingencies. (14 words)

CONCISE: This report explains accounting for loss contingencies. (7 words)

WORDY: This is to acknowledge receipt of your letter of June 1. (11 words)

CONCISE: Thank you for your letter of June 1. (8 words)

WORDY: This is to inform you that we are sending a check in the amount of $798.14. (16 words)

CONCISE: We're sending a check for $798.14. (6 words)

In summary, clear, readable writing contains no unnecessary or dead words. Be concise—your writing will be more forceful.

CLARITY

Concise writing is also clearer writing, because important ideas are not buried in unnecessary words and details. Writing as simply as possible will also help you achieve clarity, since you'll be using words the reader knows and feels comfortable with.

Other techniques for improving the clarity of your writing include the careful use of jargon and precise, concrete word choices.

Jargon

Jargon is "The specialized or technical language of a...profession."[3] We all know what accounting jargon is. It's words and phrases like *amortization, accrual, debit, GAAP,* and *deferred income taxes.*

One kind of jargon is acronyms: words composed of the first letter of a group of words, such as FASB, GAAP, and LIFO. The general rule for acronyms is to write out the words of the acronym the first time you use it, with the acronym in parentheses:

> One of the earliest groups to set accounting standards was the Committee on Accounting Procedure (CAP).

After you have identified the acronym fully, you can use the acronym alone throughout the rest of the document. If you're sure that your readers will be familiar with an acronym, and if you're writing an informal document, it's usually acceptable to use the acronym without writing it out.

Unless you use jargon, including acronyms, carefully, it will detract from the clarity of your writing.

Two guidelines can help you decide when to use jargon and when to look for other words. The first is to remember the needs of your readers, and to use language that they will understand. Another accountant will probably understand what you mean by *straight-line depreciation,* but managers or clients who have not studied accounting may be unfamiliar with the term. But be careful when using jargon even with your accounting colleagues. Would everyone with a degree in accounting know what you mean by an *operating lease?*

The second guideline for the use of jargon is to remember always to keep your word choices as simple as possible. Avoid jargon when ordinary language will say what you mean. For example, why say "the bottom line" if you mean net income or loss?

Of course, jargon is often unavoidable when you need to communicate technical information as efficiently as possible. But once again, remember the needs of your readers: define or explain technical terminology with which they may not be familiar.

Use jargon only when your readers understand it.
Define technical terms when necessary.

Precise Meaning

One of the most important elements of clear writing is precision. That is, word choices are accurate and sentences are constructed so that their meaning is clear. Precision is particularly important in accountants' writing, because accountants are often legally responsible for the accuracy of what they write. Moreover, the technical nature of accounting makes precise writing a necessity. One rule for an effective writing style is, thus, precision.

Be precise—avoid ambiguous and unclear writing.

Word Choices.   Imprecise writing can result from several causes. One culprit is poor diction, or the inaccurate use of words:

The major *setback* of the current method is that it is inefficient.
(Poor diction. The writer meant *drawback*.)
The advantage of measurements in terms of replacement costs is that the costs reflect *what the item is worth*.
(What is the precise meaning of the italicized phrase? *Worth* is vague.)

In these examples the diction problems are italicized:

POOR DICTION: The users of our financial statements may see the decline in our revenues and become *worrisome.*
REVISED: The users of our financial statements may see the decline in our revenues and become worried.
POOR DICTION: Our advertising expense, which is 1 percent of total sales, is a *negligent* amount.
REVISED: Our advertising expense, which is 1 percent of total sales, is a negligible amount.
POOR DICTION: The reason for this purchase was to *help from* liquidating LIFO layers.
REVISED: The reason for this purchase was to prevent the liquidation of LIFO layers.
POOR DICTION: This memo will discuss how to account for the *theft* of the filling station.
(This sentence says that the filling station itself was carried off.)
REVISED: This memo will discuss how to account for the robbery at the filling station.

Unclear, awkward writing can also result from the misuse of words ending in *-ing.*

AWKWARD AND UNCLEAR: The lease does not meet the 90 percent test, therefore classifying the lease as an operating lease.
REVISED: The lease does not meet the 90 percent test, so it must be classified as an operating lease.
AWKWARD AND UNCLEAR: By forming larger inventory groups, the chances of liquidating an early LIFO layer are reduced.

REVISED: Larger inventory groups reduce the chances of liquidating an early LIFO layer.
(Note: This revision also changes the sentence from
passive to active voice—see the discussion of passive
voice later in this chapter.)

AWKWARD AND UNCLEAR: In finding out this information, we will have to be
thorough in our asking of questions of the concerned
parties.

REVISED: To find out this information, we must thoroughly
question the concerned parties.

Faulty Modifiers.   Another cause of imprecise writing is misplaced and
dangling modifiers. With a misplaced modifier, the modifying word or phrase is
not placed next to the sentence element it modifies. The result is confusing sentences:

Periodic inventory systems are often used by businesses that sell a large volume
of inexpensive items *like grocery stores and drugstores.* (The italicized phrase appears
to modify *items,* but it really modifies *businesses.*)

Revised:

Periodic inventory systems are often used by businesses such as grocery stores and
drugstores, which sell a large volume of inexpensive items.

Consider another sentence with a misplaced modifier:

This technique identifies tax returns for audits with a high probability of error.

Revised:

This technique identifies, for audit, tax returns with a high probability of error.

Dangling modifiers, which usually come at the beginning of a sentence, do
not modify any word in the sentence. Usually the word modified is implied, rather
than stated directly. Look at this sentence:

After buying the bonds, the market price will fluctuate.

The writer probably meant something like this:

After we buy the bonds, the market price will fluctuate.

Here's another example:

As a successful company, disclosure of quarterly profits will attract investors.

One possible revision:

Because we are a successful company, disclosure of our quarterly profits will attract
investors.

Pronoun Reference.   Faulty pronoun reference can also cause writing to be ambiguous and confusing:

> Capitalization of interest is adding interest to the cost of an asset under construction which increases its book value.

The meaning of this sentence is unclear. What increases book value? The pronoun *which* is confusing; its reference is vague. Here is one possible revision:

> Capitalization of interest is adding interest to the cost of an asset under construction. The result is an increase in the asset's book value.

Faulty pronoun reference can be labelled *vague, ambiguous,* or *broad.* These terms all mean that the writer doesn't make clear what the pronoun refers to. The pronoun *this* is particularly troublesome:

FAULTY REFERENCE: Last year Excelsor Company changed from FIFO to LIFO and created a LIFO reserve. Because of *this,* the company decided to reduce inventories.

REVISED: Last year Excelsor Company changed from FIFO to LIFO and created a LIFO reserve. Because of this change, the company decided to reduce inventories.

FAULTY REFERENCE: The use of generally accepted accounting principles does not always produce the true financial position of a company. This is a problem for the FASB.

REVISED: The use of generally accepted accounting principles does not always produce the true financial position of a company. This weakness in the principles is a problem for the FASB.

A good rule is never to use *this* by itself. Add a noun or phrase to define what *this* is.

Another pronoun that can cause problems with reference is *it*:

FAULTY REFERENCE: The inventory valuation can follow the physical flow of goods, but it is not necessary.

REVISED: The inventory valuation can follow the physical flow of goods, but this correspondence is not necessary.

Misplaced and dangling modifiers and faulty pronoun reference are grammatical problems, and will be discussed further in Chapter 5. However, writing can be grammatically correct and still be imprecise. Consider this sentence:

> The major drawback of the current value method is verifiability.

Revised:

> The major drawback of the current value method is *the lack of* verifiability.

The revision makes quite a difference in meaning!

Often, the ability to write precisely is a function of precise reading—and thinking. An accounting professor assigned his Accounting 801 students two papers for the quarter. He then wrote the following statement on the board:

> An Accounting 801 student who completes the course will write a total of two papers this quarter. True or false?

The precise thinkers in the class realized that the statement might not be true. The students could write papers for other classes as well. Thus, some students could write *more* than a total of two papers for the quarter.

Learn to analyze carefully what you read. Then you will be able to perfect your own writing so that your meanings are clear and precise.

Here are some other examples of sentences revised to improve their clarity:

UNCLEAR: This bond is not considered risky because it sells at only 70 percent of its maturity.

REVISED: The selling price of this bond, which is 70 percent of its maturity value, does not necessarily indicate that the bond is risky.

UNCLEAR: When purchasing bonds at a discount, the investment cost is less than the face value of the investment.

REVISED: When bonds sell at a discount, the investment cost is less than the face value of the investment.

UNCLEAR: When reviewing the prior auditor's workpapers, no recognition of a possible obsolescence problem was found.

REVISED: When we reviewed the prior auditor's workpapers, we found no recognition of a possible obsolescence problem.

UNCLEAR: Historical cost accounting has several problems which do not consider inflation and changing prices.

REVISED: Historical cost accounting causes several problems because it does not take into account inflation and changing prices.

Concrete, Specific Wording

Chapter 3 discussed the use of concrete facts, details, and examples as a way to develop paragraphs. Writing that is concrete and specific adds clarity to your documents and makes them much more interesting to your readers.

Concrete writing can be explained by defining its opposite, abstract writing. Abstract writing is vague, general, or theoretical. It is hard to understand because it is not illustrated by particular, material objects. Concrete writing, on the other hand, is vivid and specific; it brings a picture into the mind of the reader.

Illustrations of abstract and concrete writing styles will make them easier to understand.

ABSTRACT
Historical cost is important in accounting. It is easy for accountants to use, and it is often seen in the financial statements. Historical cost has some disadvantages, but it has its good points, too.

CONCRETE

Historical cost often refers to the amount of money actually paid for an object at the time it was purchased. For example, if a truck was purchased in 1992 for $10,000, then $10,000 would be the truck's historical cost. Many accountants favor historical cost accounting because the values of assets are easy to determine from invoices and other records of the original purchase.

However, in times of inflation the historical cost of an asset may not indicate its true value. For example, an acre of land bought in 1950 for $5,000 might be worth several times that amount today, but it would still be recorded in the owner's books, and the balance sheet, at its historical cost. Thus one disadvantage of historical cost accounting is that it often undervalues assets.

By giving more detailed information and specific, concrete examples of historical cost, the second paragraph makes this concept easier to understand and more interesting to read.

In the following examples, vague, abstract sentences are replaced by more concrete writing:

VAGUE: Accountants should write well.
REVISED: Accountants need to write clear, concise letters to their clients and other business associates. (This sentence replaces the vague *well* by indicating two characteristics of effective writing: clarity and conciseness. The revision also gives an example of one type of accountants' writing—letters to clients and associates.)
VAGUE: The financial statements are interesting.
REVISED: Smith Corporation's earnings statement for 1992 shows a net loss of $5,437,000.

OR

Smith Corporation's financial statements for 1992 contain information that stockholders may find alarming. For example, the earnings statement shows a net loss of $5,437,000.

The example just given illustrates a particularly effective technique you can use to make your writing concrete: you can illustrate your ideas with specific details about the situation you're discussing. That is, if you're writing about the Smith Corporation's earnings statement, as in the above example, you can add relevant details about that statement that prove your point or clarify what you mean.

By adding specific, concrete detail, you will avoid vague sentences like this one:

I believe we should disclose this expense because of comparability.

If we revise the sentence to be more specific and concrete, the meaning becomes much clearer:

I believe we should disclose the advertising expense so that this year's statements will be comparable to those of prior years.

See how specific wording improves the clarity of this sentence:

VAGUE: This liability should appear on the income statement because of materiality.
CLEAR: This liability should appear on the income statement because the amount is material.

Be concrete and specific—use facts, details, and examples.

READABLE WRITING

If your writing is interesting to read, it will almost always be clear. Lively, natural sentences hold your readers' attention and keep them involved in what you are saying, so they have an easier time understanding your ideas.

This section of the chapter will be devoted to several techniques that will make your sentences readable and clear: the use of active voice, writing with variety and rhythm, and questions of tone.

Passive and Active Voice

This technique for achieving a good writing style may seem technical, but it too will become clear after a few definitions and examples.

Use active voice for most sentences.

First of all, we should define active and passive voice. Sentences are usually written in active voice. The subject of the sentence performs the action described by the verb.

ACTIVE: Most corporations issue financial statements at least once a year.

Passive voice, on the other hand, describes action done to somebody or something by another agent; the agent is not always named in the sentence.

PASSIVE: Financial statements are issued (by most corporations) at least once a year.

This formula will help you identify most passive voice verbs:

Passive Voice = | a form of the verb *to be* | + | the past participle of another verb (usually ending in *-ed*) |

FORMS OF THE VERB *TO BE*:

is, are, were, was, been, being, be, am

TYPICAL PAST PARTICIPLES:

accrued, received, used, computed, given, kept

Sometimes passive verb phrases also contain a form of *to have* (has, have, had, having) or an auxiliary (will, should, would, must, etc.), but passive voice always contains a *to be* form plus a past participle.

Active voice sentences are often clearer than passive voice sentences. Consider these examples:

PASSIVE: Taxes were increased by 50 percent. (In this example, most readers would want to know who raised taxes.)

ACTIVE: The Labor Party increased taxes by 50 percent.

PASSIVE: Deliberate understatement of assets and stockholders' equity with the intention of misleading interested parties is prohibited.

ACTIVE: SEC regulations prohibit deliberate misstatement of assets and stockholders' equity if the intention is to mislead interested parties.

Unfortunately, writers of "officialese," especially in government, business, and research, have so badly overused passive voice that we tend to accept it as standard style. But passive voice is seldom effective—it lacks the forcefulness and clarity of active voice. Compare the following pairs of sentences:

PASSIVE: A determination has been made that the statements are in violation of GAAP.

ACTIVE: The auditors have determined that the statements are in violation of GAAP.

PASSIVE: Further research should be conducted before an opinion can be issued.

ACTIVE: The auditors should conduct further research before they issue an opinion.

PASSIVE: If reversing entries are used, the possibility of bookkeeping errors is reduced.

ACTIVE: Using reversing entries reduces the possibility of bookkeeping errors.

PASSIVE: In many college accounting courses, effective writing skills are emphasized.

ACTIVE: Many college accounting courses emphasize effective writing skills.

PASSIVE: In SAS No. 1 it is required that items such as these be disclosed in the financial statements.

ACTIVE: SAS No. 1 requires that the financial statements disclose items such as these.

PASSIVE: The second general standard of field work requires that independence, in both fact and appearance, be maintained by the auditor.

ACTIVE: The second general standard of field work requires that the auditor maintain independence in both fact and appearance.

Good writers will avoid using passive voice in most situations. They will ask themselves two questions. What is the action (verb)? Who or what is doing it (subject)?

One word of warning: avoid substituting a weak active verb for passive voice. Be particularly careful of colorless verbs like *to exist* and *to occur*. The following sentences are written in active voice, but the sentences are weak:

Capitalization of option costs on land subsequently purchased should occur.

FIFO bases itself on the assumption that the first inventory acquired is the first inventory sold.

Look for descriptive, vigorous verbs to substitute for weak verbs, or reword the sentence.

We must capitalize option costs on land subsequently purchased.

The assumption that underlies FIFO is that the first inventory acquired is the first inventory sold.

When to Use Passive Voice.   While it is usually better to write in active voice, passive voice is sometimes preferable. For example, the two sentences just above could be effectively written in passive voice:

Option costs on land subsequently purchased should be capitalized.
FIFO is based on the assumption that the first inventory acquired is the first inventory sold.

Passive voice may also be necessary to avoid an awkward repetition of sentence subjects, especially in paragraphs where the same agent is performing all the action. Or the agent may be obvious or irrelevant:

The transaction was recorded October 25.

In this sentence, it would probably not be necessary to identify the person who recorded the transaction.

Another consideration about active and passive voice is that sometimes you may want to emphasize the passive subject. For example, you would say

The XYZ Company was robbed.

rather than

Some person or persons unknown robbed the XYZ Company.

Finally, passive voice may enable you to be tactful when you must write bad news or some sort of criticism:

These figures were not calculated correctly.

This sentence doesn't say who is at fault for the erroneous calculation; here passive voice may be the most diplomatic way to identify the problem without assigning blame.

We'll talk more about writing tactfully later in the chapter.

Variety and Rhythm

Another way to make your writing natural and more readable is to add variety.

Vary vocabulary, sentence lengths, and sentence structures.
Read the writing aloud to hear how it sounds.

The purpose of sentence variety is to avoid monotony—a sing-song, awkward repetition of the same sentence rhythm, or overuse of a word or phrase. Read the following paragraph aloud:

> Financial analysts use ratios to analyze financial statements. Ratios show a company's liquidity. The current ratio shows the ratio of current assets to current liabilities. Ratios also show a company's solvency. The equity ratio is an example of a solvency ratio. It shows the ratio of owners' equity to total assets. Ratios also show profitability. The return-on-investment ratio is an example. It shows the ratio of net earnings to owners' equity.

This paragraph does not sound pleasing. In fact, it could easily lull the reader to sleep. The sentences are too similar in length and structure, and the word *ratio* is repeated too often. Let's try again:

> Ratios based on financial statements can reveal valuable information about a company to investors, creditors, and other interested parties. Liquidity ratios show whether a company can pay its debts. The quick ratio, for example, is a good indication of debt-paying ability for companies with slow inventory turnover. Ratios can also indicate a company's solvency; the equity ratio, for instance, shows the percentage of owners' equity to total assets. Investors in bonds use this figure to evaluate the safety of a potential investment. Finally, ratios can give a measure of a company's profitability, which is of special interest to potential investors. The earnings-per-share ratio is probably the most popular of the profitability ratios.

Another cause of monotonous sentences is too many prepositional phrases, particularly when they are linked together to form a chain. Look again at the sentence below. Prepositions are circled; the rest of the phrase is underlined:

There are some serious, unfortunate results (of) <u>accounting</u> based (on) <u>historical cost</u> (during) <u>times</u> (of) <u>decreasing purchasing power</u> (of) <u>the monetary unit</u>.

This sentence contains a chain of prepositional phrases five links (phrases) long. A good rule is to avoid more than two prepositional phrases in a row.

If you are not sure what prepositions are, here is a partial list:

> across, after, as, at, because of, before, between, by, for, from, in, in front of, in regard to, like, near, of, on, over, through, to, together with, under, until, up, with

Variety is an important element of readable writing because it gives sentences and paragraphs a pleasing rhythm. Read your paragraphs aloud. If you notice a word or phrase repeated too often, look for a synonym. If the sentences sound choppy and monotonous, vary their structures and lengths. Often a change in the way sentences begin will improve the rhythm of the paragraph. Add an occasional short sentence, and an occasional longer one (but be sure longer sentences are still easy to understand). And be careful of too many prepositional phrases. You don't want to bore your reader, and varied sentences are one way to keep your writing lively.

Tone

The tone of a document is the way it makes the reader feel or the impression it makes. A letter can have a formal or informal tone, be personal or impersonal. It can be apologetic, cold, humorous, threatening, arrogant, respectful, or friendly.

Vary your tone according to who the reader will be. If you are writing to a colleague who is also a good friend, you can be much more informal than if you are writing to someone you know only slightly. Be particularly careful to show respect to those who are much older than you or in higher positions of authority.

One way to decide on the proper tone of a document you are writing is to put yourself in the position of your readers and to write from their point of view. This approach is called writing with the "you attitude."

First of all, the "you attitude" requires that you be courteous. Treat your correspondent with tact, politeness, and respect. Avoid abruptness, condescension, and stuffiness—or any other form of rudeness. Here are some examples of poor tone:

> This is a complicated subject, so I have tried to simplify it for you. (This sentence is condescending; it implies that the reader may not be very bright.)
>
> I acknowledge receipt of your letter and beg to thank you. (Too formal and artificial—stuffy, in fact.)
>
> Send me that report immediately. I can't understand why it has taken you so long to prepare it. (In certain situations you might *think* this way, but you'll get better results if you write with tact and courtesy.)

The use of personal pronouns (*you, I, we*) can contribute to the "you attitude." Keep the first person singular pronouns (*I, me, my*) to a minimum; focus instead on the reader with second person (*you, your*) or, in some cases, first person plural (*we, us, our*).

A personal tone, including personal pronouns, is especially effective when the message you are conveying is good news or neutral information. However, when you must write bad news or criticize someone, it's better to be impersonal in order to be tactful. Passive voice can also make a sentence more tactful:

TACTLESS: You failed to submit the form to the IRS on time.
  BETTER: The form wasn't submitted to the IRS on time.
      OR: The IRS didn't receive the form on time.

Another guideline for an effective tone is to stress the positive—what can be done rather than what cannot:

NEGATIVE: Because you were late in sending us your tax information, we cannot complete your tax return by April 15.
POSITIVE: Now that we have the information on your taxes, we can complete your tax return. We will request an extension of the deadline so that you will not be fined for a late filing.

Finally, be honest and sincere; avoid exaggeration and flattery.

In the final analysis, the guidelines for an effective writing tone are the same as those for good relationships. Learn to view a situation from the other person's point of view, and communicate in a way that shows your empathy and respect.

Here, then, is another guideline for an effective writing style.

Write from the reader's point of view. Use tone to show courtesy and respect.

EDITING FOR STYLE
AT THE COMPUTER

The section on revision in Chaper 2 mentioned software programs that some writers use to help them edit for style. These programs will analyze your text and give you such information as the average length of your sentences and the average number of letters in your words. They may also identify passive voice constructions, cliches, and pretentious word choices. Some programs also tell you how difficult your writing is to read—that is, a readability level as determined by a formula.

Keep in mind that these programs are not completely reliable. They won't identify all the weaknesses in your writing, and some of the passages they flag are not really errors. For example, we've seen in this chapter that passive voice is sometimes preferable to active voice, yet a style analyzer may identify all passive verbs as potential problems. It takes the writer's own judgment to decide when to change the passive voice and when to let it stand.

On the other hand, some of the information given by a style analyzer can truly be helpful. For example, if the analyzer tells you that your average sentence length is twenty-five words long, you know you have a problem.

In sum, style analyzers will not automatically ensure that you write effectively, but they may point out potential problems that you should consider.

Whatever techniques you use to revise your text, take time to ensure that your prose is readable, clear, and concise. Your readers will be grateful.

This chapter on style has added nine rules to our list of effective writing techniques. We now have 16 rules.

1. **Analyze the purpose of the writing and the needs and expectations of the readers.**
2. **Organize your ideas so that your readers will find them easy to follow.**
3. **Write the draft, and then revise it to make the writing polished and correct.**
4. **Make the writing unified—all sentences should relate to the main idea, either directly or indirectly. Eliminate digressions and irrelevant detail.**
5. **Use summary sentences and transitions to make your writing coherent.**
6. **Write in short paragraphs that begin with clear topic sentences.**
7. **Develop paragraphs by illustration, definition, detail, and appeals to authority.**
8. **Be concise—make every word count.**

9. Keep it simple—simple vocabulary and short sentences.
10. Write with active verbs and descriptive nouns.
11. Use jargon only when your readers understand it. Define technical terms when necessary.
12. Be precise—avoid ambiguous and unclear writing.
13. Be concrete and specific—use facts, details, and examples.
14. Use active voice for most sentences.
15. Vary vocabulary, sentence lengths, and sentence structures. Read the writing aloud to hear how it sounds.
16. Write from the reader's point of view. Use tone to show courtesy and respect.

TEST YOURSELF

Revise the following sentences, using the techniques covered in this chapter. Answers follow.

a. Can you revise these sentences so that they are simpler and more concise? Watch for hidden verbs.

1. To determine how to account for our lease, we will make reference to *Statement of Financial Accounting Standards No. 13.*
2. The history of Elliot Industry's performance, which is marginal at best, may be an indication of solvency problems that will occur in the future.
3. A number of problems have come to light that may make it necesary for us to issue an opinion that is other than unqualified.
4. I have attempted to explain the three proposed alternatives for recording the cost of the land that has been purchased.
5. It is my recommendation that New York Corporation choose to value the asset at $95,000.

b. The meaning of these sentences is not clear. Revise them so that they are unambiguous and precise.

1. After reading the following discussion, a recommendation will present the best method for our company.
2. Each alternative has its rational for use.
3. The FASB has not officially written a pronouncement on the handling of acquisition costs.
4. Proponents claimed that the proposed legislation would provide changes from the old method of depreciation that would increase deductions and simplify computations.
5. The report was concerned with the Accelerated Cost Recovery System as modified by the Tax Act of 1986. Its purpose was. . . .

c. Identify the passive voice verbs in these sentences and revise them so they are in active voice. If necessary, invent a subject for the verb.

1. I have explained the three proposed alternatives for recording the cost of the equipment that has been purchased by our client.
2. The aging of accounts receivable is distorted by the journal entries.
3. Inventory should be controlled by the bookkeepers using the general ledger.
4. This procedure can easily be implemented by management.
5. It is recommended that finished parts inventories be physically controlled.

    d. Identify the prepositional phrases in these sentences. Where too many are linked together, revise the sentence.

1. Now that the choice of sites has been made and the expiration of options is occurring, this transaction must be recorded in the books of our firm correctly.
2. We have designed an audit program for use in future audits of the accounts receivable of ABC Company.
3. An accrual of expenses reports a more accurate picture of the operations of the current business period of the company.
4. The important issue to address in this company's situation is that of the expression of an opinion of the going concern.
5. The main problem of the staff is the determination of the cost at which to record the purchase.

    e. Read this paragraph aloud and notice how monotonous it sounds. Then revise it so that sentence lengths and structures are more varied. Note also when a word or phrase is repeated too often.

> Charter Air runs scheduled flights between several local communities. Charter Air also provides charter service for several local businesses. Charter's financial statements reveal marginal profits for the past several years. Last year Charter was forced to raise prices to compensate for increased fuel prices. These price increases and several economic downturns caused passenger volume to decline drastically. Thus 1991 was a disastrous year for Charter Air. The preliminary information showed that 1991 losses were in excess of $2,000,000. This will force Charter Air into a deficit position. The 1990 balance sheet showed a net worth of $2,000,000 with total assets of $10,000,000.[4]

TEST YOURSELF—ANSWERS

(Note: Some of the errors can be corrected in more than one way, but this key will show only one possible correction. If you recognize the error, you probably understand how to correct it.)

a.
1. To determine how to account for our lease, we will refer to *Statement of Financial Accounting Standards No. 13*.
2. Elliot Industry's history of marginal performance may indicate future solvency problems.

3. We have found several problems that may require us to issue a qualified opinion.
4. I have explained the three proposals for recording the cost of the purchased land.
5. I recommend that New York Corporation value the asset at $95,000.

b.

1. The following discussion will conclude with a recommendation of the best method for our company.
2. Each alternative has its rationale for use.
3. The FASB has not written an official pronouncement on the handling of acquisition costs.
4. Proponents claimed that the proposed legislation would provide changes from the old method of depreciation; these changes would increase deductions and simplify computations.
5. The report was concerned with the Accelerated Cost Recovery System as modified by the Tax Act of 1986. The purpose of the report was . . . .

c.

1. I have explained the three proposed alternatives for recording the cost of the equipment that our client has purchased.
2. The journal entries distort the aging of accounts receivable.
3. The bookkeepers should use the general ledger to control inventories.
4. Management can easily implement this procedure.
5. The auditors recommend that we physically control finished parts inventories.

d.

1. Now that the choice (of) sites has been made and the expiration (of) options is occurring, this transaction must be recorded (in) the books (of) our firm correctly.

   Now that we have chosen the sites and the options have expired, we must record this transaction correctly in our books.
2. We have designed an audit program (for) use (in) future audits (of) the accounts receivable (of) ABC Company.

   We have designed a program for future audits of ABC Company's accounts receivable.
3. An accrual (of) expenses reports a more accurate picture (of) the operations (of) the current business period (of) the company.

   Accrued expenses report a more accurate picture of the company's current operations.
4. The important issue to address (in) this company's situation is that (of) the expression (of) an opinion (of) the going concern.

   Before we can issue our opinion, we must decide if this company is indeed a going concern.

   Note: *to address* is an infinitive (a verb), not a prepositional phrase. However, too many infinitive phrases can also make a sentence awkward.
5. The main problem (of) the staff is the determination (of) the cost (at) which to record the purchase.

   The staff's main problem is determining the cost at which to record the purchase.

e. Charter Air runs scheduled flights between surrounding communities and provides charter service for several local businesses. According to its previous financial statements, Charter has been marginally profitable in the past several years. During the past year, Charter was forced to raise its prices to compensate for increased fuel costs. Because of these price increases and the effects of the general economic downturns, passenger volume declined drastically, making 1991 a disastrous year for the company. The preliminary information showed that 1991 losses were in excess of $2,000,000. This loss will force Charter Air into a deficit position, as the 1990 balance showed a net worth of $2,000,000 with total assets of $10,000,000.

EXERCISES

Exercise 4-1

Revise the following sentences so that they are written as simply and concisely as possible. Be alert for hidden verbs.

1. We should not make reference to that information in our report.
2. The benefits of this educational program will avail themselves to the corporation via language and letters which are fresh, accurate, and clear.
3. These techniques will provide for an increased understanding of the problem.
4. Wordiness is the problem that makes my writing ineffective.
5. As you are no doubt aware, in the economic environment of today, having these services available from a firm with experience is indispensable and quite valuable.
6. I am in need of improved writing skills.
7. In conclusion, I would like to state that I feel this seminar is an excellent opportunity.
8. There are several benefits that can come from attending the seminar.
9. Enclosed please find the information you will need to make an analysis of our inventory control.
10. This method provides proper matching of expenses to revenues.

Exercise 4-2

Review the lists of simplified word choices in Table 4-1 of this chapter. Then write a shorter and/or simpler version of the following words and phrases.

1.	i.e.	13.	maintain cost control
2.	enclosed please find	14.	the writer
3.	facilitate	15.	this is to acknowledge
4.	initiate	16.	under separate cover
5.	prior to	17.	with reference to
6.	so as to	18.	utilize
7.	the major part of	19.	transpire
8.	make a purchase	20.	investigate
9.	make an analysis	21.	in the nature of
10.	for the purpose of	22.	please be advised that
11.	in the amount of	23.	terminate
12.	optimum	24.	pursuant to your inquiry

25. failed to
26. at this point in time
27. in advance of
28. due to the fact that

29. exercise care
30. pertaining to
31. it should be noted that

Exercise 4–3

Identify the jargon in the following sentences.

1. GAAP require us to issue financials annually.
2. The FASB will issue an exposure draft on that topic next month.
3. We can issue convertible debt to improve our equity position.
4. Negative cash flows may affect our position with our creditors.
5. Credit Cash for $200.
6. The historical cost of the machinery will be easy to determine.
7. Our client must file a Schedule A with his return.
8. Because of his income this year, he will be able to recapture.
9. We must issue a qualified opinion on this audit.
10. According to SFAS 13, this lease qualifies as an operating lease.

Exercise 4–4

The meaning of the following sentences is not clear. Revise the sentences so that they are unambiguous and precise.

1. The value of the option is to buy land at a stated price.
2. The return of an investment in bonds is based on the number of years to maturity and the current market rate of interest.
3. Bonds are a unique opportunity because investors can purchase and exchange them on an exchange market.
4. The company's deficit position is due to increasing fuel prices and the company's response in increasing prices.
5. All companies incur expenses that do not provide future benefits to keep their business going to produce revenue.
6. Capitalization states that once a cost expires, we should capitalize expense.
7. Calculating the present value of the bonds' principal and future cash flows will determine our risk.
8. The riskiness of these bonds does not depend on their selling price.
9. Under LIFO the lower costs are assigned to inventory which causes the cost of inventory to decrease.
10. These financial statements upset two accounting standards.

Exercise 4–5

The following sentences are abstract or vague. Revise them, using facts, details, or examples to make them more concrete. You may need to replace one vague sentence with several concrete sentences or even a short paragraph. Alternatively, you could introduce a short paragraph with an abstraction and then develop the idea with more concrete, specific sentences. Feel free to invent details that will make the ideas more specific.

1. Internal control is important.
2. Sometimes firms keep two sets of records.
3. We must record this asset at its true value. (Hint: what is "true value"?)
4. The audit did not satisfy me.
5. The firm sold the asset for its cost. (Hint: what cost?)
6. Accounting for leases is tricky.
7. The nature of this asset requires us to capitalize it.
8. The accountant in charge of accounts receivable is not doing his job.
9. These stocks look like a good buy.
10. Accountants must use good judgment.

Exercise 4-6

Identify the passive-voice constructions in the following sentences and revise them to active voice. Be careful not to substitute weak active verbs for passive voice. For some sentences you may need to invent a subject for the active verb.

EXAMPLE

PASSIVE: That alternative could have been followed.
ACTIVE: We (or the firm, our client, McDonough Corporation, etc.) could have followed that alternative.

1. Our earnings statement was distorted by these incorrect figures.
2. The option kept the land available until a decision was reached.
3. No audit work was performed on internal control by our firm.
4. Most journal entries are reviewed by accounting management.
5. The opinion to be issued on the 1992 financial statements must be qualified by our firm.
6. Although our computer was purchased last year, it is already obsolete.
7. Each month our company's net income is reduced by accrued expenses.
8. At the seminar guidelines will be provided for lease accounting.
9. The income to be reported on the 1992 financial statements must be verified by us.
10. The second general standard of auditing requires that independence, both in fact and appearance, be maintained by the auditor.

Exercise 4-7

Identify the prepositional phrases in the following sentences. Where too many phrases are linked together, revise the sentence.

EXAMPLE:

The problem of Breland Company is solved through the selection of one of the accounting methods presented.

Prepositional phrases identified:

The problem (of) Breland Company is solved (through) the selection (of) one (of)the accounting methods presented.

REVISED:

One of these accounting methods should solve Breland Company's problem.

1. The effect on our audit report of the sale of the assets is twofold.
2. The calculation of the present values of the principal of the bonds and their cash flows will reveal our risk.
3. The amortization of the discount of the bond will allow us to realize the cash flows of the bond at an even rate throughout the life of the bond.
4. The determination of the net income of the company will pose no problem for the accountants in our department.
5. An increase in advertising will make the market more aware of the products of the company.
6. The controller of the company called a meeting at 3:00 P.M. to discuss the annual report for this year.
7. The income tax return for Mr. Jones was filed on Friday.
8. Personnel of the corporation were pleased to learn of the increase in their salaries this year.
9. Representatives from the division in Ohio met for a meeting in the morning.
10. Clients of our firm are concerned about the new regulations for income taxes.

Exercise 4-8

Read the following paragraph aloud; note its monotonous rhythms. Then revise the paragraph so that it shows greater variety in sentence structures and lengths. Note also when words or phrases are repeated too often.

> Every business sells products that may be returned. The customers may be unhappy with the product for many reasons. The customer may not like the size, style, or color. The customer may also simply change his or her mind. The supplier (vendor) calls these sales returns. The customer calls them purchase returns. Such merchandise returns are minor for manufacturers and wholesalers. Such returns are major for retail department stores. Marshall Field's or Macy's may have returns of 12 percent of gross sales.[5]

NOTES

1. George deMare, *How to Write and Speak Effectively* (New York: Price Waterhouse, 1958), p. 9.
2. Ibid., p. 11.
3. William Morris, ed., *The American Heritage Dictionary of the English Language,* New College Edition (Boston: Houghton Mifflin Company, 1979), p. 701.
4. Adapted from Doug Hertha, "Audit Report of Charter Air" (unpublished student paper, University of Georgia, 1982).
5. Adapted from Charles T. Horngren, *Introduction to Financial Accounting,* 3rd ed. (Englewood Cliffs, N.J.: Prentice-Hall, Inc., 1987), p. 214. Reprinted by permission.

5

STANDARD ENGLISH
Grammar, Punctuation, and Spelling

One way to improve the clarity of your writing is to use standard English. Standard English has been described as follows:

> There are two broad varieties of written English: standard and nonstandard. These varieties are determined through usage by those who write in the English language. Standard English...is used to carry on the daily business of the nation. It is the language of business, industry, government, education, and the professions. Standard English is characterized by exacting standards of punctuation and capitalization, by accurate spelling, by exact diction, by an expressive vocabulary, and by knowledgeable usage choices.[1]

A mastery of standard English tells the reader much about you as a person and as a professional. Your use of correct grammar says that you are an educated person who understands and appreciates the proper use of our shared language.

A grammatically correct document, free of mechanical and typographical errors, also shows that you know the importance of detail and are willing to spend the time necessary to prepare an accurate, precise document.

This chapter presents some of the most commonly made errors in grammar, punctuation, and spelling. Of course, only a few principles can be covered in this short space, so you should consult a basic English handbook for a complete list of rules and explanations. The discussion here focuses on rules that give accountants the most trouble.

MAJOR SENTENCE ERRORS

Major sentence errors include three kinds of problems: fragments, comma splices, and fused sentences. These errors are very distracting to readers and often interfere seriously with their ability to understand the meaning of the sentence.

Fragments

A sentence fragment is just what its name suggests: part of a sentence. You may recall that every sentence needs two essential elements, a subject and a verb. Often with sentence fragments, one of these elements is left out. Here are some examples:

> To account for the transaction correctly.
> For example, *Statement of Accounting Concepts No. 13*.
> The reason being that we must cut costs in the shipping department.
> (*Being* is a present participle;* it cannot be substituted for a complete verb like *is* or *was*.)
> Although, our new computer system makes billing much faster.
> (This dependent clause has a subject and verb, but it cannot stand alone as a sentence because it is introduced by a subordinate conjunction, *although*.)

Comma Splices

The second type of major sentence error is the comma splice, which occurs when independent clauses are combined by a comma alone.

An independent clause is a group of words with a subject and a verb; it can stand alone as a sentence. Here are two independent clauses punctuated as separate sentences:

> Increases in assets are recorded as debits on the left side of a T-account. Decreases are recorded as credits on the right side.

Sometimes writers want to combine two independent clauses into one sentence. This can be done correctly in several ways:

1. Put a semicolon (;) between the clauses.
   Increases in assets are recorded as debits on the left side of a T-account; decreases are recorded as credits on the right side.
2. Combine the clauses with a comma and a coordinating conjunction (*and, but, for, or, nor, yet, so*).
   Increases in assets are recorded as debits on the left side of a T-account, and decreases are recorded as credits on the right side.
3. Combine the clauses with a semicolon, a conjunctive adverb, and a comma. (Conjunctive adverbs include *however, therefore, thus, consequently, that is, for example, nevertheless, also, furthermore, indeed, instead, still*.)
   Increases in assets are recorded as debits on the left side of a T-account; however, decreases are recorded as credits on the right side.

*Consult a grammar handbook for explanations of technical grammatical terms such as this.

Study the following comma splices. The independent clauses are joined by a comma alone:

COMMA SPLICE:	LIFO may result in a lower net income, therefore, a company has lower income tax liabilities.
REVISED:	LIFO may result in lower net income; therefore, a company has lower income tax liabilities.
COMMA SPLICE:	Accountants write many letters as part of their professional responsibilities, for example, they may write letters to the IRS.
REVISED:	Accountants write many letters as part of their professional responsibilities. For example, they may write letters to the IRS.
COMMA SPLICE:	These transactions were not recorded correctly, that is, they were not recorded in the proper accounts.
REVISED:	These transactions were not recorded correctly; that is, they were not recorded in the proper accounts.

Fused Sentences

Fused sentences, which are also called run-on sentences, occur when two independent clauses are joined without any punctuation at all:

FUSED SENTENCE:	Generally accepted accounting principles are not laws passed by Congress however, the Code of Professional Ethics requires accountants to follow GAAP.
REVISED:	Generally accepted accounting principles are not laws passed by Congress. However, the Code of Professional Ethics requires accountants to follow GAAP.
FUSED SENTENCE:	This equipment is not a long-term asset it can be expensed rather than capitalized.
REVISED:	This equipment is not a long-term asset; it can be expensed rather than capitalized.

PROBLEMS WITH VERBS

The correct use of verbs is a complicated matter in any language, as you will appreciate if you have ever studied a foreign language. Fortunately, because English is the native language for most of us, we usually use verbs correctly without having to think about them. We just know what sounds right.

Several problems do tend to occur even in the writing of educated people. We will now look briefly at a few of those problems.

Tense and Mood

The *tense* of a verb reflects the time of the action described by the verb:

PAST TENSE:	We *signed* the contract.
PRESENT TENSE:	We *are signing* the contract.
	OR
	Do we *sign* the contract now?
	OR
	Everyone *signs* the contract.

FUTURE TENSE: We *will sign* the contract next week.

Usually the choice of tense is logical and gives writers few problems.

The *mood* of a verb, however, is a little more confusing than its tense. Three moods are possible: indicative (states a fact or asks a question), imperative (a command or request), and subjunctive (a condition contrary to fact). The subjunctive mood causes the most trouble, although we often use it without realizing it:

If I *were* you, I would attend the seminar.
(condition contrary to fact)

The most common use of the subjunctive is to follow certain verbs such as *recommend, suggest,* and *require:*

I recommend that the company *depreciate* the asset over five years.
I suggest that he *meet* with the sales representatives next week to discuss the problem.
The SEC requires that we *disclose* that item in our financial statements.

One problem to avoid is an unnecessary shift in tense or mood:

TENSE SHIFT: Sales *dropped* by 20 percent last year. That drop *is* the result of increased competition. (Shift from past to present tense.)
REVISED: Sales dropped by 20 percent last year. That drop was the result of increased competition.
MOOD SHIFT: We *must credit* Cash to account for this transaction. Then *debit* Office Supplies. (Shift from indicative to imperative mood.)
REVISED: We must credit Cash to account for this transaction; then we must debit Office Supplies.
OR
We must credit Cash and debit Office Supplies to account for this transaction.
MOOD SHIFT: If we *increase* inventory, we *would service* orders more quickly. (Shift from indicative to subjunctive.)
REVISED: If we increase inventory, we will service orders more quickly.
OR
If we increased inventory, we would service orders more quickly.
MOOD SHIFT: If we *changed* our policy, we *will attract* more customers. (Shift from subjunctive to indicative.)
REVISED: If we changed our policy, we would attract more customers.
OR
If we change our policy, we will attract more customers.

Subject-Verb Agreement

Another major problem with verbs is subject-verb agreement. A verb should agree with its subject in number. That is, singular subjects take singular verbs; plural subjects take plural verbs. Note that singular verbs in the present tense usually end in *s*:

That (one) <u>man</u> <u>works</u> hard.

Those (two) <u>men</u> <u>work</u> hard.

Some irregular verbs (*to be, to have,* etc.) look different, but you will probably recognize singular and plural forms:

That <u>stock</u> <u>is</u> a good investment.

These <u>stocks</u> <u>are</u> risky.

The ABC <u>Corporation</u> <u>has</u> fifty accountants on its staff.

Some <u>corporations</u> <u>have</u> net earnings of more than a million dollars.

There are a few difficulties with this rule. First, some singular subjects are often thought of as plural. *Each, every, either, neither, one, everybody,* and *anyone* take singular verbs:

<u>Each</u> of the divisions <u>is</u> responsible for maintaining accounting records.

Second, sometimes phrases coming between the subject and the verb make agreement tricky:

The <u>procedure</u> used today by most large companies in their foreign divisions <u>is</u> explained in this article.

Finally, two or more subjects joined by *and* take a plural verb. When subjects are joined by *or,* the verb agrees with the subject closest to it:

Either <u>Company A or Company B</u> <u>is</u> planning to issue new stocks.

Either the <u>president or the managers</u> <u>have</u> called this meeting.

PROBLEMS WITH PRONOUNS

Two common problems with pronouns are agreement and reference. Understanding what is meant by agreement is easy: a pronoun should agree with its antecedent (the word it stands for). Thus singular antecedents take singular pronouns, and plural antecedents take plural pronouns:

Mr. Jones took *his* check to the bank.

Each *department* keeps *its* own records.

This rule usually gives trouble only with particular words. Note that *company, corporation, firm, management,* and *board* are singular; therefore, they take singular pronouns.

The *company* increased *its* profits by fifty percent. (Not *company—their*.)

The Accounting Principles *Board* discussed accounting for intangible assets in *its* Opinion No. 17. (Not *Board—their*.)

Management issued *its* report. (But: The *managers* issued *their* report.)

The second problem with pronouns is vague, ambiguous, or broad reference. This problem was discussed in Chapter 4, but here are some additional examples:

FAULTY REFERENCE: Although our trucks were purchased last year, this year's revenue depends on them. *This* associates the true cost with this year's revenues.

REVISED
(one possibility):   Although our trucks were purchased last year, this year's revenue depends on them. To associate the true cost with this year's revenue, we must apply the matching principle.

FAULTY REFERENCE: Adjusting entries are needed to show that an expense has been incurred, but that it has not been paid. *This* is a very important step.

REVISED: Adjusting entries are needed to show that an expense has been incurred, but that it has not been paid. Making these adjusting entries is a very important step.

While agreement and reference cause writers the most problems with pronouns, occasionally other questions arise.

One of these questions is the use of first and second person, which some people have been taught to avoid. In the discussion of tone in Chapter 4 we saw how the use of these personal pronouns can contribute to an effective writing style for many documents. Personal pronouns are not usually appropriate, however, in formal documents such as some reports and contracts.

There are a few other cautions about the use of personal pronouns. First, use first person singular pronouns (*I, me, my, mine*) sparingly to avoid writing that sounds self-centered. The second problem to avoid is using *you* in a broad sense to mean people in general, or as a substitute for another pronoun:

INCORRECT: I don't want to file my income tax return late because the IRS will fine *you*.

REVISED: I don't want to file my income tax return late because the IRS will fine me.

Pronouns and Gender

In the English language, there are no singular personal pronouns that refer to an antecedent that could be either masculine or feminine. Until about a generation ago, the masculine pronouns (*he, him, his*) were understood to stand for either gender:

Each *taxpayer* must file *his* tax forms by April 15.

A sentence like this one was standard, even though the antecedent for the pronoun (in this case, *taxpayer*) could be either male or female.

Most people today believe that this older pronoun usage is no longer appropriate. They prefer the use of nonsexist language, including pronouns that are gender neutral, unless, of course, the antecedent is clearly male or female.

The *controller* of Excel Corporation was pleased with *his* company's progress. (The controller is a man.)

OR

The *controller* of Excel Corporation was pleased with *her* company's progress. (The controller is a woman.)

When the pronoun's antecedent is not clearly male or female, most people write sentences like these:

Each *taxpayer* must file *his or her* tax forms by April 15.

Each *taxpayer* must file *his/her* tax forms by April 15.

Unfortunately, the *he or she* or *he/she* constructions can be awkward, especially if several occur in the same sentence:

Each *taxpayer* must file *his or her* tax forms by April 15, unless *he or she* has filed for an extension.

What is the solution? The best approach for most sentences is to use plural nouns and pronouns:

All *taxpayers* must file *their* tax forms by April 15, unless *they* have filed for an extension.

There will be occasions, though, when you can't use plurals, and then you will have to use your best judgment to decide which pronoun to use. But keep these guidelines in mind:

1. Most of today's business publications use nonsexist language, including pronouns that are gender neutral. If you use the older style, your writing may seem outdated.
2. Some of your readers may be annoyed by a choice of pronouns that seems to be gender biased.
3. Perhaps the most important guideline, however, is to write what your readers expect.

PROBLEMS WITH MODIFIERS

Chapter 4 discussed the two main problems that can occur with modifiers: (1) misplaced modifiers, which occur when the modifier is not placed next to the word it describes, and (2) dangling modifiers, which do not modify any word in the sentence:

MISPLACED MODIFIER:	We only sold five service contracts last year. (*Only* is misplaced. It should be next to the word or phrase it modifies.)
REVISED:	We sold only five service contracts last year.
DANGLING MODIFIER:	When preparing financial statements, GAAP must be adhered to.
REVISED:	When preparing financial statements, we must adhere to GAAP.

The best guideline for using modifiers correctly is to place them next to the word or phrase they describe.

PARALLEL STRUCTURE

Parallel sentence elements are those that are grammatically equal: nouns, phrases, clauses, etc. When these items appear in a list or a compound structure, they should be balanced. Nouns should not be matched with clauses, for example, nor sentences matched with phrases:

STRUCTURE NOT PARALLEL:	This report will discuss the system's purpose, how much it costs, and its disadvantages.
	(This sentence combines a noun, a dependent clause, and another noun.)
REVISED:	This report will discuss the system's purpose, cost, and disadvantages.
STRUCTURE NOT PARALLEL:	We recommend the following procedures:

- Hire a consultant to help us determine our needs. (phrase)
- Investigate alternative makes and models of equipment. (phrase)
- We should then set up a pilot program to test the new system. (sentence)

REVISED:	We recommend the following procedures:

- Hire a consultant to help us determine our needs. (phrase)
- Investigate alternative makes and models of equipment. (phrase)
- Set up a pilot program to test the new system. (phrase)

APOSTROPHES AND PLURALS

The rules for apostrophes and plurals are quite simple, but many people get them confused.

Most plurals are formed by adding either *s* or *es* to the end of the word. If you are unsure of a plural spelling, consult a dictionary.

With one exception, apostrophes are never used to form plurals. Apostrophes are used to show possession. For singular words the form is *'s*. For plural words the apostrophe comes after the *s*:

SINGULAR	**PLURAL**
firm's capital	officers' salaries
statement's figures	users' interests
business's profits	businesses' profits

A commonly made mistake is *stockholder's equity*. When stockholder(s) is plural (it usually is), the apostrophe comes after the *s: stockholders' equity*.

There is one exception to the plural-apostrophe rule. Abbreviations, numerals, and letters can form their plurals with *'s:*

1990's or 1990s
CPA's or CPAs

Often a phrase requiring an apostrophe can be rewritten using *of* or its equivalent:

the company's statements (the statements of the company)
the month's income (the income of the month)
a week's work (the work of a week)
the year's total (the total for the year)

And note these possessive plurals:

two companies' statements
five months' income
three weeks' work
ten years' total
prior years' statements

"Ten years' total" might also be written "ten-year total." But analyze the difference in meaning between "ten-year total" and "ten years' totals."

Finally, some writers confuse *it's* with *its. It's* is a contraction of *it is; its* is the possessive pronoun:

It's important to make careful journal entries.
The company issued its statements.

COMMAS

Commas are important because they can make sentences easier to understand. For example, the meaning of this sentence is ambiguous:

I would not worry because you appear to have a thriving business.

Adding a comma will clear up the confusion:

> I would not worry, because you appear to have a thriving business.

Comma Guidesheet

USE COMMAS:
1. before *and, but, or, not, for, so,* and *yet*—when these words come between independent clauses.
   The FASB issued a Discussion Memorandum, and many accountants responded with their opinions.
   Competition increased, but we still increased our earnings.
2. following an introductory adverbial clause.
   When investors read a company's financial statements, they are especially interested in the net income figure.
   Because production costs are up, we will be forced to raise our price.
   Although we worked all night, the report was still late.
   If we increase our inventory, we will need a new warehouse.
3. following transitional expressions and long introductory phrases.
   In *Statement of Financial Accounting Standards No. 2* (SFAS No. 2), the FASB defined its position on research and development costs.
   To improve our sales in the southeast region, we are adding three new sales representatives. However, we still need four more representatives.
4. to separate items in a series (including coordinate adjectives).
   Accounting students must be intelligent, dedicated, and conscientious.
   Send this report to the vice president, the manager of the shipping department, and the senior bookkeeper.
5. to set off nonrestrictive clauses and phrases (compare rule 4, in the following section).
   The SEC, which is an agency of the federal government, is concerned with proper presentation of financial statements.
   The annual report, which was issued in June, contained good news for investors.
   The main office, located in Boston, employs 350 people.
6. to set off contrasted elements.
   Treasury stock is a capital account, not an asset.
   We want to lower our prices, not raise them.
7. to set off parenthetical elements.
   Changes in accounting methods, however, must be disclosed in financial statements.
   "Our goal," he said, "is to dominate the market."

DO NOT USE COMMAS:
1. to separate the subject from the verb or the verb from its complement.
   Incorrect:
   The company that manufactures trucks, has an impressive net income.
   Correct:
   The company that manufactures trucks has an impressive net income.
2. to separate compound verbs or objects.
   Incorrect:
   She wrote angry letters to the FASB, and the SEC.

Correct:
She wrote angry letters to the FASB and the SEC.

3. to set off words and short phrases that are not parenthetical.

   Incorrect:
   Financial transactions are recorded, in journals, in chronological order.

   Correct:
   Financial transactions are recorded in journals in chronological order.

4. to set off restrictive clauses, phrases, or appositives (compare rule 5 in the preceding section).

   Incorrect:
   A problem, that concerns many accountants, is the use of historical cost in times of inflation.

   Correct:
   A problem that concerns many accountants is the use of historical cost in times of inflation.

5. before the first item or after the last item of a series (including coordinate adjectives).

   Incorrect:
   Some asset accounts are noncurrent, such as, land, buildings, and equipment. (The faulty comma is the one before *land*.)

   Correct:
   Some asset accounts are noncurrent, such as land, buildings, and equipment.

COLONS AND SEMICOLONS

The rules for colons (:) are few and easy to master, although sometimes writers use them incorrectly. Used correctly—and sparingly—colons can be effective because they draw the readers' attention to the material that follows.

Colons can be used in the following situations:

1. to introduce a series.
   Three new CPA firms have located in this area recently: Smith and Harrison, CPAs; Thomas R. Becker and Associates; and Johnson & Baker, CPAs.
2. to introduce a direct quotation, especially a long quotation that is set off from the main body of the text.
   The senior partner issued the following instructions:
   "All audit workpapers should include concise, well-organized memos summarizing any problem revealed by the audit."
3. to emphasize a summary or explanation.
   My investigation of Ace Manufacturing's financial situation led me to an important conclusion: unless Ace attracts new capital immediately, it may be forced into bankruptcy.
4. following the salutation in a business letter.
   Dear Mr. Evans:

When a colon introduces a series, an explanation, or a summary, the clause that precedes the colon should be a complete statement:

We have increased our sales to the following customers: Elliot Industries, Anderson, Inc., and Trueblood Manufacturing.

Not

Our best customers are: Elliot Industries, Anderson, Inc., and Trueblood Manufacturing.

Semicolons (;) are used for only two situations: between independent clauses (see page 74) and between items in a series, if the items themselves have internal commas:

The proposal was signed by John Underwood, President; Alice Barret, Vice-President; and Sue Barnes, Treasurer.

DIRECT QUOTATIONS

The punctuation of direct quotations depends on their length. Short quotations (less than five typed lines) are usually run-in with the text and enclosed with quotation marks. Longer quotations are set off from the text—indented and single spaced—with no quotation marks. Direct quotations should be formally introduced; a colon may separate the introduction from the quoted material. Study the following examples:

SFAS No. 14 defines an industry segment as a "component of an enterprise engaged in providing a product or service or a group of related products or services primarily to unaffiliated customers...for a profit."[2]

SFAS No. 14 gives the following definition of an industry segment:
Industry segment. A component of an enterprise engaged in providing a product or service or a group of related products and services primarily to unaffiliated customers (i.e., customers outside the enterprise) for a profit. By defining an industry segment in terms of products and services that are sold primarily to unaffiliated customers, this Statement does not require the disaggregation of the vertically integrated operations of an enterprise.[3]

A direct quotation requires a citation identifying its source. It's also better to identify briefly the source of a quotation within the text itself, as the above examples illustrate. If a quotation comes from an individual, use his or her complete name the first time you quote from this source:

According to Richard Smith, an executive officer of the Fairways Corporation, "The industry faces an exciting challenge in meeting foreign competition."

Notice the placement of punctuation in relation to quotation marks:

Inside quotation marks:

period	quotation."
comma	quotation,"

Outside quotation marks:

colon	quotation":
semicolon	quotation";

Inside or outstide quotation marks:

question mark ?" or "?
—depending on whether the question mark is part of the original quotation:

Mr. Misel asked, "Where is the file of our new client?"

Did Mr. Misel say, "I have lost the file of our new client"?

One final remark. Sometimes writers depend too heavily on direct quotation. It's usually better to paraphrase—to express someone else's ideas in your own words—unless precise quotation would be an advantage. As a rule, no more than ten percent of a paper should be direct quotation. To be most effective, quotations should be used sparingly, and then only for authoritative support or dramatic effect.

SPELLING

Finished, revised writing should be entirely free of misspelled words. Keep a dictionary on your desk, and use it if you have any doubt about a word's spelling. Or, if you are using a word processor, use a spelling check program to eliminate misspelled words.

Spelling: If in doubt, look it up!

The following short list contains words commonly misspelled or misused by accountants:

accrual, accrued
advise/advice
affect/effect
cost/costs, consist/consists, risk/risks
led, misled
occurred, occurring, occurrence
principal/principle
receivable, receive
separate, separately

The italicized words in the following sentences are frequently confused:

> Please *advise* us of your decision. (*Advise* is a verb.)
> We appreciate your *advice*. (*Advice* is a noun.)
> This change in accounting policy will not *affect* the financial statements. (*Affect* is a verb.)
> This change in accounting policy will have no *effect* on the financial statements. (*Effect* is usually a noun. Rarely, *effect* is a verb meaning "to cause to happen.")
> The *cost* of the new machine is more than we expected. (*Cost* is singular.)
> The *costs* of these assets are not recorded correctly. (*Costs* is plural, but when you say the word aloud, you can't hear the final *s*.)
> The ambiguous footnote may *mislead* investors. (*Mislead* is present or future tense.)
> This ambiguous footnote *misled* investors. (*Misled* is past tense.)
> How should we record the *principal* of this bond investment?
> This procedure does not follow generally accepted accounting *principles*.

HELP FROM THE COMPUTER

Some writers check their text for grammatical errors by using a grammar check software program. These programs can help you identify some problems with grammar including errors with verbs, pronouns, and punctuation. But as with programs that analyze writing style, these computer aids may not catch all your grammatical errors, and they may flag as an error a usage that is indeed correct. Thus the decision to use grammar checkers to review your text is really a matter of personal experience and preference: some excellent writers praise them highly, but others find them of limited use.

A word processor with a good spelling check program is another matter. As we've pointed out numerous times throughout preceding chapters, any corrections you make are much easier when the document is prepared with a word processor. Spelling check programs are also a tremendous help in correcting spelling and typographical errors.

In summary, standard English—including correct grammar, punctuation, and spelling—is essential for polished, professional writing. Don't just guess about the rules; resolve your uncertainties with a grammar handbook, dictionary, or grammar check computer program. Remember the needs of your readers. Correct grammar and mechanics are necessary for smooth, clear reading.

A final word: Be sure to proofread your finished product for typographical errors—whether you or someone else does the actual typing. Typographical errors make work look sloppy, and the writer seem careless. Effective writing should look professional: correct, neat, and polished.

This chapter has given another rule for effective writing. We now have 17.

1. **Analyze the purpose of the writing and the needs and expectations of the readers.**
2. **Organize your ideas so that your readers will find them easy to follow.**

3. Write the draft, and then revise it to make the writing polished and correct.
4. Make the writing unified—all sentences should relate to the main idea, either directly or indirectly. Eliminate digressions and irrelevant detail.
5. Use summary sentences and transitions to make your writing coherent.
6. Write in short paragraphs that begin with clear topic sentences.
7. Develop paragraphs by illustration, definition, detail, and appeals to authority.
8. Be concise—make every word count.
9. Keep it simple—simple vocabulary and short sentences.
10. Write with active verbs and descriptive nouns.
11. Use jargon only when your readers understand it. Define technical terms when necessary.
12. Be precise—avoid ambiguous and unclear writing.
13. Be concrete and specific—use facts, details, and examples.
14. Use active voice for most sentences.
15. Vary vocabulary, sentence lengths, and sentence structures. Read the writing aloud to hear how it sounds.
16. Write from the reader's point of view. Use tone to show courtesy and respect.
17. Proofread for grammar, punctuation, spelling, and typographical errors.

TEST YOURSELF

Identify and correct the errors in the following exercises, using the guidelines discussed in this chapter. Answers follow.

a. Identify and correct fragments, comma splices, or fused sentences. Some sentences are correct.

1. The controller argued that these costs do not provide future benefits, thus, she decided to expense them.
2. Ethel Corporation must not only improve its internal control system it must also review its procedures for accounts receivable.
3. Many types of users rely on financial statement information, for example, creditors use the information to evaluate a firm's credit worthiness.
4. Physical volume is one factor that affects cost behavior; other factors include efficiency, changes in technology and unit prices of inputs.
5. The main reason for our concern, however, is the incorrect recording of accounts receivable.

b. Some of these sentences have verb errors: subject-verb agreement or shifts in tense or mood. Identify these errors and correct the sentences.

1. Changes in the general purchasing power of the dollar forces accountants to deal with an unstable monetary unit.
2. If we improve our financial ratios, investors would find our stock more attractive.
3. Neither the president nor the supervisors understand the new policy.

4. One problem we found in our reviews of the records were that revenues were not always recorded in the proper period.

5. A statement with supplementary disclosures provide additional information to investors.

c. Correct any pronoun errors you find in the following sentences.

1. When an investor or creditor wishes to compare two companies, they cannot always rely on the historical cost statements for the comparison.

2. Ace Manufacturing should remember that they are allowed to expense the cost of certain property.

3. The FASB deals with research and development costs in their *Statement of Financial Accounting Standards No. 2.*

4. Management is interested in improving the revenue figures for their report to the stockholders.

5. Each accountant is required to complete their report on time.

d. Revise the following sentence for parallel structure.

We recommend the following improvements in your system of internal controls:

- The controls over cash should be strengthened.
- An accounting manual to ensure that transactions are handled uniformly.
- Improved documentation of accounting procedures.

e. Punctuate the following sentences correctly.

1. When the Board of Directors met in December the company showed a net loss of $5 million.

2. To increase the revenues from its new product the company introduced an advertising campaign in New York Chicago and Los Angeles.

3. The biggest problem in our firm however is obsolete inventories.

4. We currently value our inventories according to LIFO not FIFO.

5. For example Elixir Products should consider the FASB's *Statement No. 13* which deals with leases.

TEST YOURSELF—ANSWERS

(Note: Some of the errors can be corrected in more than one way. For most sentences, this key will show only one possible correction. If you recognize the error, you probably understand how to correct it.)

a.
1. Comma splice. Correction:
   The controller argued that these costs do not provide future benefits; thus, she decided to expense them.

OR

The controller argued that these costs do not provide future benefits. Thus, she decided to expense them.

2. Fused sentence. Correction:
   Ethel Corporation must not only improve its internal control system; it must also review its procedures for accounts receivable.

3. Comma splice. Correction:
   Many types of users rely on financial statement information; for example, creditors use the information to evaluate a firm's credit worthiness.

4. Correct.

5. Correct. (*However* doesn't come between two independent clauses in this sentence.)

b.

1. Subject-verb agreement. Changes in the general purchasing power of the dollar force accountants to deal with an unstable monetary unit. (The verb should agree with the subject *changes*.)

2. Mood shift. If we improve our financial ratios, investors will find our stock more attractive.

   OR

   If we improved our ratios, investors would find our stock more attractive.
   (The original sentence contained a shift in mood from indicative to subjunctive. Either mood is correct here; the key is to be consistent.)

3. Correct.

4. Subject-verb agreement. One problem we found in our reviews of the records was that revenues were not always recorded in the proper period. (The verb should agree with *problem*.)

5. Subject-verb agreement. A statement with supplementary disclosures provides additional information to investors. (The verb should agree with *statement*.)

c.

1. When an investor or creditor wishes to compare two companies, he or she cannot always rely on the historical cost statements for the companies. (Alternative: *investors or creditors/they*).

2. Ace Manufacturing should remember that it is allowed to expense the cost of certain property.

3. The FASB deals with research and development costs in its *Statement of Financial Accounting Standards No. 2.*

4. Management is interested in improving the revenue figures for its report to the stockholders.

5. Each accountant is required to complete his or her report on time. (Alternative: *All accountants/their*.)

d. We recommend the following improvements in your system of internal control:
   - stronger controls over cash
   - an accounting manual to ensure that transactions are handled uniformly
   - improved documentation of accounting procedures.

e.

1. When the Board of Directors met in December, the company showed a net loss of $5 million.

2. To increase the revenues from its new product, the company introduced an advertising campaign in New York, Chicago, and Los Angeles.

3. The biggest problem in our firm, however, is obsolete inventories.

4. We currently value our inventories according to LIFO, not FIFO.
5. For example, Elixir Products should consider the FASB's *Statement No. 13,* which deals with leases.

EXERCISES

Exercise 5-1

Join these independent clauses together in three ways.

under variable costing a company's sales will influence income
under absorption costing both sales and production will affect income

Exercise 5-2

Identify and correct fragments, comma splices, or fused sentences. Some sentences are correct.

1. The department had added several new employees, thus, we had a training session.
2. To increase sales; therefore, we tried a new advertising campaign.
3. However, not all committee members agreed with the president.
4. Tax season is our busiest time of the year everyone works long hours.
5. Because everyone worked extra hours, we were able to finish on time.
6. Although, the reason for our decreased sales is not obvious.
7. The reason for our low inventory turnover being that this is our slow season.
8. Accountants do not depreciate land, therefore, we cannot allocate land costs on a systematic and rational basis.
9. Historical cost usually results from arms'-length transactions and therefore provides reliable measures of transactions.
10. Although we discussed this policy at the May meeting, some staff members still do not understand it.

Exercise 5-3

Some of these sentences have verb errors: subject-verb agreement or shifts in tense or mood. Identify these errors and correct the sentences.

1. If we hired a consultant, we will be able to design a new system.
2. Either the auditors or the controller is responsible for this report.
3. One of our biggest problems are a lack of adequate controls.
4. The physical flow of goods generally follow the FIFO pattern.
5. Each of these statements is prepared according to GAAP.
6. Neither the president nor the controller understand the new policy.
7. We will depreciate this asset over ten years. First, however, determine its salvage value.
8. The future benefits provided by the bond is partly due to its high interest rate.
9. Restating asset values to current costs results in realized and unrealized holding gains and losses.

10. We review the client's system of internal control. Then we will recommend ways to improve it.

Exercise 5-4

Correct any pronoun errors you find in the following sentences.

1. According to the IRS, each taxpayer must sign his tax form when he files his income tax return.
2. The company increased their revenues last year.
3. Three new procedures were used to improve the internal control system. This was the responsibility of Nancy Copeland.
4. Although accountants often use reversing entries to reduce the possibilities of error, they are not essential parts of the accounting process.
5. The trouble with our new system is that you have so much trouble understanding it.
6. The Smallwood Corporation has greatly increased it's advertising expense.
7. A switch to LIFO usually results in a lower income tax liability and a lower inventory figure on the balance sheet; this would be important to our company.
8. The Board of Directors will hold its next meeting in July.
9. Every corporation coming under SEC regulations must follow certain procedures in preparing their financial statements.
10. Everyone registering for the convention will receive a package of information when they arrive.

Exercise 5-5

Revise the following sentences for parallel structure.

1. Send the memo to these people:
   * the internal auditor
   * the manager of the marketing department
   * you should also send a copy to the president.
2. This committee will study the problem, a recommendation for correcting it, and oversee the correction procedure.
3. The hiring decisions will be based on three criteria: experience, training, and whether the applicants have good communication skills.

Exercise 5-6

a. Complete the following chart.

SINGULAR	SINGULAR POSSESSIVE	PLURAL	PLURAL POSSESSIVE
statement			
company			
business			
cost			
risk			
CPA			
year			
industry			

b. Use the words from the chart to fill in these sentences. The singular form of the correct word is given in the parentheses.

1. (CPA) _____ from all over the country will be at the convention.
2. (business) Investors examine a _____ statements to determine its financial condition.
3. (cost) Record all these _____ in the proper amounts.
4. (statement) Which of the _____ is in error?
5. (cost) What is the replacement _____ of this machine?
6. (risk) Investors in these bonds must accept certain _____ .
7. (industry) Research and development are crucial in many _____ .
8. (year) We should see a profit in two _____ time.
9. (company) The Board of Directors considered the _____ pension plan.
10. (statement) We are making changes in the two _____ totals.

Exercise 5–7

Punctuate the following sentences correctly.

1. Most companies base asset values on their historical cost, however, there are exceptions to this rule.
2. To provide this important information to the users of our financial statements we should include supplementary disclosures.
3. The report was filed February 12 1992 in Washington D.C.
4. Before we can issue an opinion on these financial statements we must be sure that this transaction was recorded correctly.
5. The report was signed by the controller the internal auditor and the vice president.
6. The auditors revealed several problems in Thompson Company's financial records such as its depreciation policy its handling of bad debts and its inventory accounting.
7. The presidents letter contained the following warning "If our revenues don't increase soon the plant may be forced to close"
8. "We're planning a new sales strategy" the manager wrote in reply.
9. We have decided not to invest in the Allied bonds at this time instead we are considering Blackstone's common stocks.
10. Although our revenues increased during June expenses rose at an alarming rate.

Exercise 5–8

Identify and correct any misspelled words in the following list. Look up any words you are unsure of; not all of these words were included in the chapter.

1. believe
2. receive
3. occured
4. seperate
5. accural

6. benefitted
7. existance
8. principle (the rule)
9. cost (plural)
10. mislead (past tense)
11. advise (the noun)
12. affect (the verb)

NOTES

1. Charles T. Brusaw, Gerald J. Alred, and Walter E. Oliu, *The Business Writer's Handbook,* 3rd ed. (New York: St. Martin's Press, 1987), p. 220.
2. *Statement of Financial Accounting Standards No. 14: Financial Reporting for Segments of a Business Enterprise* (Stamford, Conn.: Financial Accounting Standards Board, 1976), para. 10a. Copyright by Financial Accounting Standards Board, High Ridge Park, Stamford, Connecticut, 06905, U.S.A. Reprinted with permission. Copies of the complete document are available from the FASB.
3. Ibid.

6

FORMAT FOR CLARITY
Document Design

How a document looks at first glance can make a big difference in how the reader reacts to it. An attractive document generally gets a positive response, but a paper that is not pleasing to the eye may never be read.

This chapter looks at techniques of document design that will make your letters, memos, and reports more attractive. But a good design will do more for the readers than appeal to them visually. A well-planned format will also contribute to the clarity of your documents by making them easier to read.

Later chapters will cover the conventions and formats specific to particular kinds of documents, such as the standard parts of a letter, memo, or report. The techniques covered in this chapter will be those you can use for any kind of document you write. We'll consider ways to make your documents look professional and attractive, such as the choice of paper and print, and the use of white space. We'll also see how techniques of formatting, such as headings, lists, and graphic illustrations, can make your documents clearer and more readable.

A PROFESSIONAL APPEARANCE

If you already work for an organization, you may find models of well-designed documents by looking at papers written by other people with whom you work. In fact, your employer may expect all documents to be written a certain way—in a standard format, for example, and on the company's letterhead and standard stock paper. You will seem more professional if you learn your employer's expectations for document design and then adhere to them.

Often, however, whether you're on the job or still in school, you will have a fair amount of leeway in how you design your documents. The remainder of this chapter will look at techniques you can use to give your documents a professional appearance. For example, a professional-looking document uses high-quality materials—the best paper and the best print. It incorporates an attractive use of margins and white space, and it is perfectly neat.

Paper and Print

If you're already employed, you may not have any choice about the paper; you will probably use your company's letterhead stationery and standard stock for all your documents. If you are still a student, however, you will need to select a paper that makes a good impression. Use $8\frac{1}{2} \times 11$-inch paper of a high quality bond, about 24-pound weight, in white or off-white. Never use erasable bond paper because it smears too easily.

The print of your document is another consideration. If you are using a word processor, you will need a letter-quality printer for a professional appearance. If you're using a typewriter, be sure that it produces a clean, even type. And whether you use a typewriter or a printer, be sure to use a good ribbon.

A number of type styles are available on both typewriters and printers. Choose a standard type style, never a novelty style or one that simulates handwriting. The type size is also important. Most people find larger type easier to read.

White Space and Margins

White space is that part of a page which does not have any print. White space includes margins, the space between sections, and the space around graphic illustrations.

A document with visual appeal will have a good balance between print and white space. White space also makes a document easier to read. The space between sections, for example, helps the reader to see the paper's structure.

There are no hard-and-fast rules for margin widths or the number of lines between sections. As a general guideline, however, plan about a one-inch margin for the sides and bottoms of your papers. The top of the first page should have about a two-inch margin; subsequent pages should have a one-inch margin at the top.

Leave an extra line space between the sections of your document. A double-spaced page, for example, would have three lines between sections.

For any document that is single spaced, be sure to double space between paragraphs.

Neatness Counts!

Whatever you write, the final copy should be error-free and extremely neat. Of course a word processor, especially one with a spelling checker, enables you to find errors and make corrections with ease. If you are using a typewriter, corrections should be few and unobtrusive. Sloppiness in a document seems unprofessional and careless.

FORMATTING

Some writers think of the format of their document only in terms of straight text: page after page of print unbroken by headings or other divisions. Yet if you look at almost any professional publication, including this handbook, you will see how various formatting devices, such as headings, lists, and set-off material, make pages more attractive and easier to read.

Headings

For any document longer than about half a page, headings are useful to divide the paper into sections. Headings make a paper less intimidating to readers because the divisions break up the text into smaller chunks. In a sense, headings give readers a chance to pause and catch their breath.

Headings also help the readers by showing them the structure of the paper and what topics it will cover. In fact, many readers preview the contents of a document by skimming through it to read the headings. For this reason, headings should be worded so that they indicate the contents of the section to follow. Sometimes headings suggest the main idea of the section, but they should clearly identify the topic discussed. If you look through this book, you will see how headings suggest the content of the chapters. Chapter 1 even uses questions for headings, which is a good technique if not overused.

Headings can be broken down into several levels of division. Some headings indicate major sections of a paper, while other headings indicate minor divisions. In other words, a paper may have both headings and subheadings. Earlier in this chapter, for example, "A Professional Appearance" indicates a major section of the chapter; "Paper and Print" marks the beginning of a subtopic, because it is just one aspect of a document's appearance. Generally, a short document needs only one level of heading, but this rule can vary depending on what you are writing about.

The style of the heading, how the heading is placed and printed on the page, varies with the levels of division. Some styles indicate major headings; other styles indicate subheadings.

Here are four heading styles and the levels of division.

FIRST LEVEL: CENTERED, ALL CAPS

Second Level: Centered, Underlined

Third Level: Centered, Not Underlined

Fourth Level: Left Margin, Underlined

If you use fewer than four levels, your headings may be in any style, as long as they are in descending order. For example, you might use second-level headings for main topics and fourth-level headings for subtopics. If you are using only one level of headings, any style is acceptable.

It's possible to overuse headings. You would not, for example, put a heading for every paragraph.

Lists and Set-off Material

Another formatting technique that can make a document easier to read is set-off material, especially for lists. Mark each item on the list with a number, a "bullet," or some other marker. Double space before and after the list and between each item, but single space the items.

Here is an example using bullets:

Your firm might use data processing equipment in at least five additional areas:

- budgets
- payrolls
- fixed assets
- accounts payable
- accounts receivable

Set-off lists not only improve the appearance of the paper by providing more white space, but they may also be more readable. The following example presents the same information as straight text and in a list format. Which arrangement do you prefer?

Special journals increase our efficiency. They do this by providing a greater division of labor. Also, they cut down on the time needed to post transactions. Finally, they give us quick and easy access to important financial information.

Special journals increase our efficiency because they

- provide a greater division of labor
- reduce the time needed to post transactions
- give us easy access to important financial information

The letter in Figure 7–3 shows other examples of set-off lists.

Occasionally you will use set-off material for other purposes besides lists. For example, long direct quotations are set off; they are indented and single spaced. Very rarely, you will set off a sentence or two for emphasis. Chapters 2–6 use this technique to emphasize the guidelines for effective writing.

Pagination

The next formatting technique is a simple one, but it's overlooked surprisingly often. For every document longer than one page, be sure to include page numbers. They can be placed at either the top or the bottom of the page, be centered, or be placed in a corner. Begin numbering on page 2.

Graphic Illustrations

Graphic illustrations, such as tables, charts, or graphs, can sometimes make a document more interesting and informative. Tables or charts are an efficient way to present and summarize numerical data, and graphs are useful for comparisons. The graph in Figure 6–1 compares the earnings trends for three departments over a five-year period.

If you include graphics, number them, and given them a descriptive title. Graphic illustrations should be labeled sufficiently so that they are self-explanatory, but they should also be discussed within the text of the document. This discussion should refer to the illustration by name and number (for example, *Figure 6–1*). The discussion should appear in the text before the illustration. The illustrations can be placed either in the body of the document, close to the place in the text where they are discussed, or in an appendix.

If you are using an illustration with a lot of numbers, you may need to use a highlighting technique, such as bold face type, to make the most significant figures stand out.

FIGURE 6–1   A graph used to compare earnings trends.

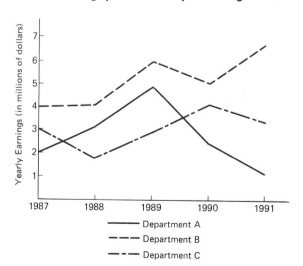

DOCUMENT DESIGN AT THE COMPUTER

Many of the formatting techniques we've talked about in this chapter are easily done with a word processor. For example, word processors make it easy to change margins, arrange set-off materials, add white space, and design headings. In addition, software programs can help you produce graphic illustrations of an excellent quality. And because the computer will make corrections to the text before you print your final draft, you will be able to submit a document that is flawless and professional.

Word processors and graphics packages may be the only computerized aids you ever need for effective document design. You should be aware, though, that with the advent of desktop publishing it is possible to produce documents that look as if they've been typeset with very elaborate equipment. For example, desktop publishing offers a wide variety of typefaces, graphics designs, and other options for page layouts.

For some documents, such as formal reports that will have a wide readership, it may be wise to use desktop publishing programs. They can make your documents look like professional publications and thus may give you a competitive advantage when you need it most.

This chapter has completed the rules for effective writing.

1. **Analyze the purpose of the writing and the needs and expectations of the readers.**
2. **Organize your ideas so that your readers will find them easy to follow.**
3. **Write the draft, and then revise it to make the writing polished and correct.**
4. **Make the writing unified—all sentences should relate to the main idea, either directly or indirectly. Eliminate digressions and irrelevant detail.**
5. **Use summary sentences and transitions to make your writing coherent.**
6. **Write in short paragraphs that begin with clear topic sentences.**
7. **Develop paragraphs by illustration, definition, detail, and appeals to authority.**
8. **Be concise—make every word count.**
9. **Keep it simple—simple vocabulary and short sentences.**
10. **Write with active verbs and descriptive nouns.**
11. **Use jargon only when your readers understand it. Define technical terms when necessary.**
12. **Be precise—avoid ambiguous and unclear writing.**
13. **Be concrete and specific—use facts, details, and examples.**
14. **Use active voice for most sentences.**
15. **Vary vocabulary, sentence lengths, and sentence structures. Read the writing aloud to hear how it sounds.**
16. **Write from the reader's point of view. Use tone to show courtesy and respect.**
17. **Proofread for grammar, punctuation, spelling, and typographical errors.**
18. **Use formatting techniques to give your writing clarity and visual appeal.**

EXERCISES

Exercise 6-1

Collect examples of effective and ineffective formatting—personal correspondence as well as professional publications. How could the ineffective documents be improved?

Assume you are the supervisor of your company's accounting department. Write a memo to the staff suggesting ways they might improve the design of the documents they write. Use some of the examples you've found to illustrate your memo.

Exercise 6-2

Choose a paper you've already written for a class assignment or on the job. Revise the paper, using at least two of these techniques:

- headings
- set-off list
- graphic illustrations
- improved use of white space

7

LETTERS

Accountants write many letters—to clients, government agencies, fellow professionals, and so on. They may write letters seeking data about a client's tax situation, for example, or information needed for an audit. They may also write letters to communicate the results of research into a technical accounting problem. Other typical letters written by accountants are engagement letters and management advisory letters.

For any letter to get the best results, of course, it must be well written.

This chapter will begin with some basic principles of good letter writing—organization, style, tone, and format. Then we'll look at some of the typical kinds of letters accountants write.

BASIC PRINCIPLES
OF LETTER WRITING

Effective letters have many of the characteristics of other good writing—tight organization, correct grammar and mechanics, and an active, direct style. They should be, in other words, coherent, clear, and concise. Letters should also be neat and attractive.

Coherent Organization

Letters can vary in length from one paragraph to several pages, although many business letters are no longer than a page. But whatever the length, you should be certain about what you want to include before you begin; then you won't forget something important.

As with other writing tasks, you'll need to analyze the purpose of your letter before you write it. If you are answering another person's letter, it will help to have that letter before you and note any comments for which a reply is needed. Finally, jot down a brief outline to organize the material logically.

It's also important to think about who the reader of your letter will be, especially when you are writing about a technical topic. The knowledge and experience of your readers will determine how detailed the explanations of technical material will be.

Sometimes, for example, you will need to explain complex accounting procedures in words a nonaccountant could understand. *Tax Research Techniques,* a study published by the AICPA, discusses user needs in writing letters to clients about tax problems:*[1]

> Like a good speaker, a good writer must know the audience before beginning. Because tax clients and their staff vary greatly in their tax expertise, it is important to consider their technical sophistication when composing a tax opinion letter. The style of a letter may range from a highly sophisticated format, with numerous technical explanations and citations, to a simple composition that uses only layperson's terms. In many situations, of course, the best solution lies somewhere between the two extremes.

Like other kinds of writing, letters are organized into an introduction, a body, and a conclusion. Each section uses summary sentences to emphasize main ideas and help the reader follow the train of thought.

The *introduction* of a letter identifies the subject of the letter or the reason the letter was written. You may also need to mention previous communciation on the subject, such as an earlier letter or phone call. The introduction should also summarize briefly the main ideas and/or recommendations discussed in your letter. If your letter is very long, it's also a good idea to identify in your introduction the main issues or topics the letter will cover.

The *body* of the letter is divided logically into discussions of each topic. Arrange the topics in descending order of importance: start with the most important issue and work your way down to the least important. Begin the discussion of each issue with a summary sentence stating the main idea or recommendation.

Paragraphs should be short, usually a maximum of four or five sentences, and each one should begin with a topic sentence.

The letter's *conclusion* may be a conventional courteous closing:

Thank you very much for your help.

*Copyright © 1989 by the American Institute of Certified Public Accountants, Inc.

The conclusion is also a good place to tell your correspondent exactly what you want him or her to do, or what you will do to follow up on the subjects discussed in the letter:

> May I have an apppointment to discuss this matter with you? I'll be in Chicago next week, October 7–12. I'll call your secretary to set up a time that is convenient for you.

If your letter is very long, your conclusion may also summarize your main ideas and recommendations.

Conciseness and Clarity

Conciseness and clarity, qualities of all good writing, are particularly important in letters. You don't want to waste your readers' time, nor do you want them to miss important ideas. Come to the point quickly, and say it in a way they will be sure to understand.

A number of the techniques already presented in this handbook are useful in achieving short, clear letters. For example, you will want your writing to be unified—paragraphs with a central idea that is easy to spot. You will also want the letter to be as brief and simple as possible, while still conveying an unambiguous, precise meaning.

Tone

One of the most important characteristics of a well-written business letter is its tone, or the way it makes the reader feel. Chapter 4 discussed writing with the "you attitude," which means that you write from the point of view of your readers, emphasizing their interests and needs. Courtesy and respect are also important qualities of business letters—as, indeed, they are in all forms of communciation.

In general, effective letters will reflect a personal, conversational tone. However, the best tone to use for a given letter depends to some extent on the purpose and reader of that letter. Review the discussion of tone in Chapter 4 to see how the content of your letter and your relationship with the reader can affect the tone you choose for your correspondence.

Form and Appearance

One of the primary characteristics of an effective letter is a neat appearance. Good stationery is important: $8\frac{1}{2} \times 11$-inch, unlined paper of a high-quality bond, about 24-pound weight. Envelopes, 4×10 inches, should match the stationery.

Business letters should be typed, or printed on a letter-quality printer. Corrections should be few and unobtrusive. Neatness is essential!

A letter is usually single spaced, with double spacing between paragraphs, although letters can be double spaced throughout (see the sample format in Figure 7-1). Margins should be at least one inch on all sides and as even as possible, although the length of the letter will affect the margin width.

One-page letters should be placed so that the body of the letter, excluding the heading, is centered on the page or slightly above center. A word processor makes it easy to experiment with margins and spacing until you get the best arrangement.

Study the diagram in Figure 7-1. This diagram identifies the parts of a letter and their proper placement. Remember also that formatting techniques, such as headings and set-off lists, can make your letters attractive and easy to read.

Parts of the Letter

Heading.   The heading contains your address (not your name) and the date of the letter. If you use letterhead stationery, center the date under the printed heading or place it next to the right margin.

Inside Address.   The inside address is a reproduction of the address on the envelope. Place the title of the person to whom you are writing either on the same line as his or her name, or on the following line:

Anna M. Soper, President
Muffet Products
516 N. 25th Street
Edinburg, TX 78539

Anna M. Soper
Director of Personnel
Muffet Products
516 N. 25th Street
Edinburg, TX 78539

It's usually better to address a letter to a specific person, rather than to an office or title. You can find the name of the person to whom you are writing by phoning the company or organization.

Salutation.   If possible, address your correspondent by name:

Dear Ms. Soper:
        or
Dear Mr. Smith:

For a woman correspondent, use *Ms.* unless she prefers another title.

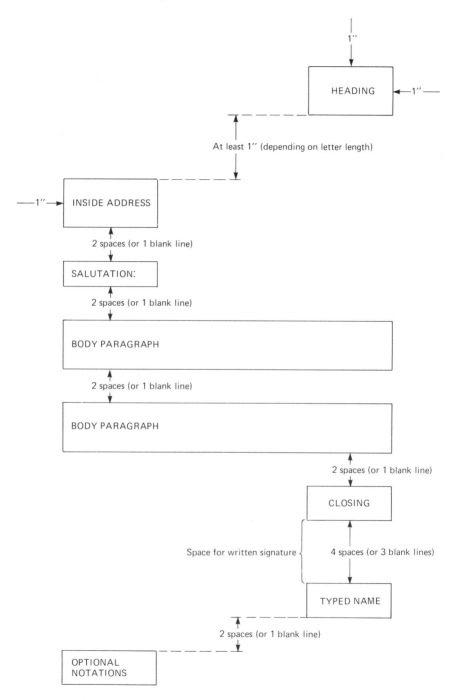

FIGURE 7-1. Diagram of a Letter Format.

If you know your correspondent well, you may want to use his or her first name in the salutation:

Dear Anna:

Be careful with the use of first names, however, especially when you are writing to an older person or one in a higher position of authority than you are. In many situations, a respectful, courteous tone requires the use of a title and last name.

If you don't know the name of your correspondent, you can use a salutation such as the following:

Dear Director of Personnel:
Dear Sir or Madam:

Note that a colon (:) always follows the salutation.

Closing.   The formal closing of a letter, which usually is placed next to the right margin, comes immediately above the signature. Capitalize the first word, and put a comma after the closing. Any of the following closings is correct:

Sincerely yours,
Sincerely,
Yours very truly,
Very truly yours,

Signature.   Your name should be printed four lines below the closing; your position can be placed beneath your name. The space between the closing and printed name is for your handwritten signature:

Sincerely,

Anna M. Soper

Anna M. Soper
President

Optional Parts of a Letter.   Sometimes you will need additional notations below the signature, on the left margin. First, if someone else types your letter, a notation is made of your initials (all capital letters) and the typist's (all lower case):

AMS:lc
or
AMS/lc

Second, if the letter includes an enclosure, make a notation:

Enclosure(s)

Finally, if you will distribute copies of the letter to other people, note this fact:

cc: John Jones

Second Page.   Many business letters are only one page long. If you need to write additional pages, each one should have a heading identifying the addressee, the date, and the page number. This information is usually printed at the left margin:

Mr. Richard Smith
November 18, 1992
Page 3

RESPONDING TO CORRESPONDENCE

When you reply to a letter written by someone else, it's important to respond in a way that will build a good working relationship between you and your correspondent. Many of the techniques for effective letters already discussed apply to responses. Here is a summary of those techniques, as well as a few pointers that apply particularly when you are answering someone else's letter:

1. Respond promptly—by return mail if possible.
2. Reread carefully the letter you received, noting questions that need answers or ideas that need your comment.
3. For the opening paragraph:
   - Refer to earlier correspondence, such as the date of the letter you received.
   - If your letter is good news, or at least neutral, state clearly and positively the letter's main idea.
   - If your letter contains bad news, such as the denial of a request, identify the subject of the letter in the opening paragraph. State the explicit refusal later in the body of the letter, after you have prepared the reader with some buffer material.
4. Answer all your correspondent's questions fully and cover all relevant topics in sufficient detail. At the same time, your letter should be as concise as possible.
5. End with a courteous closing.

TYPICAL ACCOUNTING LETTERS

Before we begin this section, we should note that many accounting firms have standardized letters for some situations. For example, the management of a firm may have decided on the organization and even the specific wording that it requires its staff to use for engagement letters, management advisory letters, and the like.

If your firm uses standardized letters, you will simply adapt the basic letter to the specific case you are concerned with, adding dates, names, figures, and other relevant facts.

Presented below are sample letters for various situations, along with some general comments on the content and organization of these letters.

Engagement Letters

Engagement letters put into writing the arrangements made between an accounting firm and a client. Engagement letters can confirm the arrangements for a variety of services—audit, review, compilation, management advisory services, or tax. The main advantage of an engagement letter is that it clarifies the mutual responsibilities of accountant and client and thus prevents possible misunderstandings.

Engagement letters can vary a great deal in content, depending on the firm writing the letter, the type of services to be provided, and the facts of the case. However, most engagement letters have three basic elements:

- a description of the nature and limitations of the service that the accountants will provide
- a description of the reports that the accounting firm expects to issue
- a statement that the engagement will possibly not disclose errors, irregularities, or illegal acts.[2]

In addition to these elements, an engagement letter may also include other information, such as important deadlines for the work; assistance that the client will provide, such as providing certain records and schedules; information about the fee; and a space for the client to indicate acceptance of the arrangements outlined in the engagement letter.

Figure 7–2 shows a sample engagement letter for an audit.

Management Advisory Letters

At the conclusion of an audit, an accountant often writes a letter to the client suggesting ways the client can improve the business. This type of letter may contain suggestions on a variety of topics. For example, the letter may include recommendations for improving

- internal control
- the accounting and information system
- inventory control
- credit policies
- budgeting
- tax matters
- management of resources
- operating procedures

```
                          Brown and Wynne
                   Certified Public Accountants

201 W. Tenth Street                              Austin, Texas  78712


                              July 15, 1992


     Mr. George Smith
     Heritage Manufacturing Company
     301 Planters Road
     Austin, Texas  78712

     Dear Mr. Smith:

          This letter will confirm the arrangements we discussed for the
     audit of Heritage Manufacturing Company for the year ended December
     31, 1992.

          The purpose of the audit will be to examine Heritage Company's
     financial statements for the year ended December 31, 1992.  Our
     examination will be conducted in accordance with generally accepted
     auditing standards, and we will use the tests and procedures necessary
     to express an opinion on the fairness of the financial statements.
     As part of our audit, we will review the internal control system
     and conduct tests of transactions.  Although these procedures may
     disclose material errors or illegal acts, a possibility remains
     that we may not discover irregularities during the course of the
     audit.

          At the close of our examination, we will issue our report on
     the audit.  We will also prepare your federal and state income tax
     returns for the year ended December 31, 1992.  Both the audit re-
     port and the tax returns should be complete about March 15, 1993.

          Our fees will be at our regular rates, based on the time re-
     quired to perform these services.  We will bill you when we have
     completed the work.

          If you accept the arrangements outlined in this letter, please
     indicate your acceptance by signing in the space below and sending
     us the attached copy of this agreement.

          We are pleased that you have appointed us to be your auditor,
     and we look forward to working with you and your staff.


                              Sincerely,

                              Carla Brown

                              Carla Brown, CPA

     Accepted by:
     Date:
```

FIGURE 7-2 Engagement Letter for An Audit.

Sometimes, if the auditor includes many recommendations in the management letter, the letter may be quite long. If you write a management letter that is over three pages, consider organizing it into a report with a transmittal letter. Address the transmittal letter to the president or board of directors of the client's company, and summarize in the letter the major recommendations made in the report.

In any case, whether the management letter is a single document or a report with a transmittal letter, remember that long letters are more attractive and easier to read if they contain headings. These headings will divide the letter into logical sections.

Whatever the format of your management letter, write it so that it will be helpful to your client and build a good professional relationship between the client and your firm. The techniques for effective writing discussed so far in this book are certainly applicable to management letters: clear and logical organization, readable style, and specific and concrete explanations.

In an article in the *Journal of Accountancy,* Robert T. Lanz and S. Thomas Moser noted that management letters often anger clients because the letters don't give enough specific information to support the accountants' suggestions.[3] Lanz and Moser stress the importance of answering three questions about each recommendation:

- Why is the change needed?
- How can it be accomplished?
- What benefits will the client receive?

In addition, Lanz and Moser note that the letter should be well organized, with key points summarized near the beginning. The authors conclude their article with a brief discussion about the style of management letters:

> Auditors may tend to write management letters in a perplexing combination of "legalese" and "accountantese." If this is what our clients are getting, we should put aside the technical jargon and verbosity and write a readable letter that makes good sense...[4]

An example of a short but effective management advisory letter appears in Figure 7-3. The recommendations included in this letter are taken from Lanz and Moser's article.[5]

Tax Research Letters

Accountants who provide tax services often write letters to their clients communicating the results of the research into some tax question. These letters can be for after-the-fact or tax-planning situations.

The content and organization of these letters can vary, but *Tax Research Techniques* suggests the following basic outline:[6]*

*Copyright © 1989 by the American Institute of Certified Public Accountants, Inc.

```
                        BEASLEY AND POOLE
                    Certified Public Accountants
                        1553 W. Ellis Street
                      Atlanta, Georgia  30316


                          March 15, 1992


Mr. Robert F. Freeman, President
Southeast Manufacturing Company
24 N. Broad Street
Atlanta, Georgia  30327

Dear Mr. Freeman:

     Our examination of Southeast Manufacturing's financial statements for
the year ended December 31, 1991, revealed several areas where we believe
you could improve your business:

     °  Adoption of data processing
     °  Stronger budgeting system
     °  Review of credit policies

The following paragraphs will explain these recommendations in greater
detail.

Electronic Data Processing

Due to the large volume of paperwork processed and the complexity of related
transactions, the present manual accounting system has become unwieldy.
In this connection, we suggest that you consider using data processing
equipment in the following areas:
1.  Sales
2.  Budgets
3.  Inventories
4.  Accounts receivable and cash receipts
5.  Accounts payable and cash disbursements
6.  Payrolls
7.  Fixed assets
8.  General ledger and journal entries

Adoption of data processing in some or all of these areas would, we believe,
reduce clerical workloads, tend to keep clerical salaries at a minimum
and, most importantly, speed up bookkeeping functions in order to provide
current financial information for management decisions and to facilitate
the preparation of financial statements.
```

FIGURE 7-3 Management Advisory Letter.

Mr. Robert F. Freeman
March 15, 1992
Page 2

Budgets

Operating, selling, and general administrative expenses for 1991 as compared
with 1990 increased from $1 million to $1,050,000, a change of 5 percent.
Although management has been able to control expenditures, we believe efforts
in this area would be assisted by implementation of a strong system of
budgeting.

Under such a system, responsibility for actual performance is assigned to
employees most directly responsible for the expenditures involved. (It is
best that such employees have a role in establishing the budgets.) Periodic
reports reflecting actual and budgeted amounts, together with explanations
of significant variances, should be provided to management personnel responsible for approving the budgets initially. We cannot overemphasize the value
of sound budgeting and planning in all areas of the company's activities.

Credit Policies

The history of write-offs of bad accounts over the past few years indicates
that the write-off percentage has declined. Considering the low net earnings
margin under which the company operates (slightly less than .6 percent of net
sales), it is most important that this favorable record continue since a significant increase in bad debts could have a substantial negative impact on
net earnings.

In view of the high cost of money for business in general, management should
consider reviewing its credit policies to reasonably assure that the risk
inherent in continued sales to customers of questionable credit standing is
justified. This is a delicate area of policy; it is not desirable to so
restrict sales representatives that profitable sales would be lost because
of overly stringent credit policies. However, a reasonable amount of control
should be exercised by the credit and collection department to assure a minimum of bad accounts. For example, a limit could be set on the amount which
sales representatives could extend to customers whose accounts have reached
a certain balance.

   We will be glad to discuss these suggestions with you and help you implement them.

                              Sincerely,

                              Roger Poole

                              Roger Poole
                              Beasley and Poole
                              Certified Public Accountants

FIGURE 7-3 Continued

- the facts on which the research was based
- caution that the advice is valid only for the facts previously outlined
- the tax questions implicit in these facts
- the conclusions, with the authoritative support for the conclusions
- areas of controversy that the IRS might dispute (Tax accountants do not all agree that the letter should identify the vulnerable areas in the client's situation. *Tax Research Techniques* suggests that if the letter does identify these weaknesses, the accountant should caution the client to control access to the letter.)

In addition to a logical organization, such as the one outlined here, tax research letters should be understandable to the client. Tax questions are often highly technical, and the accountant may need to explain the conclusions in terms a business person will understand.

Figures 7-4[7]* and 7-5[8] provide two illustrations of letters written to clients to report the results of tax research. The letter in Figure 7-4, which is written to the president of a large corporation, deals with a complicated tax issue. While this letter is clearly written, it contains a great deal of technical information and terminology.

In contrast, the letter in Figure 7-5 is written much more simply. The topic is less complicated, and the letter contains fewer technical terms.

As different as these two client letters are, they are both appropriate for their readers and the purposes for which they were intended.

STANDARDIZED LETTERS: A CAUTION

As we mentioned earlier, many organizations have standardized letters that they use for situations that occur often, such as engagement letters. These form letters save time, and they also convey the message precisely and reliably. If your employer expects you to use these standardized letters, then of course you should do so.

With the wide-spread use of word processors that store documents, however, there is a danger that writers will use form letters when personalized letters would be more appropriate. If you use standardized letters, be sure that they are responsive to the reader's needs and concerns.

If you know your correspondent personally, a friendly reference to a topic of mutual interest can add warmth to your letter. The last paragraph of the letter in Figure 7-5 provides a friendly, personalized closing to a client letter:

> I'm sorry that the news from me wasn't more favorable. I look forward to seeing you, though, at the firm's holiday reception!

*Copyright ©1989 by the American Institute of Certified Public Accountants, Inc.

December 24, 1989

Mr. Red E. Ink, President
Ms. Judith Dixon, Vice President
Ready, Incorporated
120 Published Lane
Calum City, USA 00002

Dear Mr. Ink and Ms. Dixon:

This letter confirms the oral agreement of December 17, 1989, in which our firm agreed to undertake the preparation of your respective federal income tax returns along with that of Ready, Incorporated, for next year. This letter also reports the preliminary results of our investigation into the tax consequences of the formation of Ready, Incorporated, last March. We are pleased to be of service to you and anticipate that our relationships will prove to be mutually beneficial. Please feel free to call upon me at any time.

Before stating the preliminary results of our investigation into the tax consequences of your incorporation transaction, I would like to restate briefly all of the important facts as we understand them. Please review this statement of facts very carefully. Our conclusions depend on a complete and accurate understanding of all the facts. If any of the following statements is either incorrect or incomplete, please call it to my attention immediately, no matter how small or insignificant the difference may appear to be.

Our conclusions are based on an understanding that on March 1, 1989, the following exchanges occurred in the process of forming a new corporation, Ready, Incorporated. Ms. Dixon transferred two copyrights to Ready, Incorporated, in exchange for 250 shares of common stock. Ms. Dixon had previously paid $200 for filing the copyrights. In addition, the corporation assumed an $800 typing bill, which Ms. Dixon owed for these two manuscripts.

Mr. Ink concurrently transferred all the assets and liabilities of his former sole proprietorship printing company, Red Publishings, to the new corporation in exchange for 750 shares of Ready, Incorporated, common stock. The assets transferred consisted of $11,700 cash, $10,000 (estimated market value) printing supplies, $50,000 (face value) trade receivables, and $58,300 (tax book value) equipment. The equipment, purchased new in 1987 for $100,000, had been depreciated for tax purposes under the modified accelerated cost recovery system (MACRS) since its acquisition.

FIGURE 7-4 A Letter Reporting the Results of Tax Research—Sophisticated Client

Red E. Ink
Judith Dixon
December 24, 1989
Page 2

The liabilities assumed by Ready, Incorporated, consisted of the $65,000 mortgage remaining from the original equipment purchase in 1987 and current trade payables of $10,000.

We further understand that Ready, Incorporated, plans to continue to occupy the building leased by Red Publishings on May 1, 1987, from Branden Properties until the expiration of that lease on April 30, 1991.

Finally, we understand that Ready, Incorporated, has issued only 1,000 shares of common stock and that Mr. Ink retains 730 shares; that Mr. Ink's wife Neva holds ten shares; that Mr. Tom Books, the corporate secretary-treasurer, holds ten shares; and that Ms. Dixon holds the remaining 250 shares. The shares held by Mrs. Ink and Mr. Books were given to them by Mr. Ink, as a gift, on March 1, 1989.

It is our understanding that Ready, Incorporated, will report its taxable income on an accrual method, calendar-year basis.

Assuming that the preceding paragraphs represent a complete and accurate statement of all the facts pertinent to the incorporation transaction, we anticipate reporting that event as a wholly nontaxable transaction. In other words, neither of you, the incorporators (individually), nor your corporation will report any taxable income or loss soley because of your incorporation of the printing business. The trade receivables collected by Ready, Incorporated, after March 1, 1989, will be reported as the taxable income of the corporate entity; collections made between January 1, 1989, and February 28, 1989, will be considered part of Mr. Ink's personal taxable income for 1989.

There is a possibility that the Internal Revenue Service could argue (1) that Ms. Dixon is required to recognize $800 of taxable income and/or (2) that the corporation could not deduct the $10,000 in trade payables it assumed from the proprietorship. If either of you desire, I would be pleased to discuss these matters in greater detail. Perhaps it would be desirable for Mr. Bent and me to meet with both of you and review these potential problems prior to our filing the corporate tax return.

FIGURE 7-4 Continued

Red E. Ink
Judith Dixon
December 24, 1989
Page 3

If Mr. Tom Books desires any help in maintaining the corporation's regular financial accounts, we shall be happy to assist him. It will be necessary for us to have access to your personal financial records no later than March 1, 1990, if the federal income tax returns are to be completed and filed on a timely basis.

Finally, may I suggest that we plan to have at least one more meeting in my office sometime prior to February 28, 1990, to discuss possible tax-planning opportunities available to you and the new corporation. Among other considerations, we should jointly review the possibility that you may want to make an S election and that you may need to structure executive compensation arrangements carefully and may wish to institute a pension plan. Please telephone me to arrange an appointment if you would like to do this shortly after the holidays.

Thank you again for selecting our firm for tax assistance. It is very important that some of the material in this letter be kept confidential, and we strongly recommend that you carefully control access to it at all times. If you have any questions about any of the matters discussed, feel free to request a more detailed explanation or drop by and review the complete files, which are available in my office. If I should not be available, my assistant, Fred Senior, would be happy to help you. We look forward to serving you in the future.

Sincerely yours,

Robert U. Partner

FIGURE 7-4 Continued

September 19, 1992

M/M Dale Brown
2472 North Mayfair Road
Fillingham, SD 59990

Dear Dale and Rae:

Thanks again for requesting my advice concerning the tax treatment of your
interest expenses. I am sorry to report that only a portion of your expenses
can be deducted this year.

My research has uncovered a series of successes by the IRS in convincing several
important courts that interest such as yours should not be allowed as a deduction to reduce your taxes. Unfortunately, the court whose decision initially
would prevail upon us would hold against you, and a series of court hearings,
over two or three years or so, would be necessary for you to win the case.

This research has been restricted to fact situations that are similar to yours,
that is, in which the taxpayer both owns a municipal bond and owes money to
the bank from an interest-bearing loan.

It seems that the IRS would rather have you purchase the municipal bonds with
your own money, rather than with the bank's. It maintains that you get a double
benefit from the nontaxability of the School Board interest income and the
deductibility of the interest expense that is paid to the bank. Thus, that
portion of the interest that relates to the bond investment is not allowed.
A business purpose for the loan salvages the deduction, however, so you can
deduct the interest from the loan that relates to Dr. Rae's clinic.

You may just have to live with this situation, as the IRS has been winning
cases like these for over ten years. Yours is not likely to be the one that
changes their mind, so you might reconsider your investment in the municipals
in the near future.

My conclusion is based upon the facts that you have provided me, and upon the
reliability of the court cases that I found.

I'm sorry that the news from me wasn't more favorable. I look forward to seeing
you, though, at the firm's holiday reception!

Sincerely,

Ellen P. Morgan
Tax Researcher

FIGURE 7-5 A Letter Reporting the Results of Tax Research—Less Sophisticated Client

EXERCISES

Write letters for the situations described below. Use the proper format and effective organization and style. Invent any information you feel is necessary to make your letters complete.

Exercise 7-1 (all levels)

You are considering a move to a distant city, and you would like to work with a local accounting firm there. You have five years' experience working as a CPA in the city where you now live.

Write a letter requesting an interview to discuss possible employment with the firm for which you wish to work.

Exercise 7-2 (all levels)

You have prepared the federal and state income tax returns for your client, Alexander Littleton. Write a cover letter to Mr. Littleton to mail with the completed returns. In your letter include:

- a reminder for him to sign the returns on the lines checked
- the amounts that he owes in both state and federal taxes
- a reminder of the filing deadline

Exercise 7-3 (all levels)

One of your clients, Buz's Sports, has not paid for a tax return that you completed March 15. You billed the client at the time you completed the return and mailed a reminder in May. At the end of June, Buz's still hasn't paid the bill, and you need to write a letter to the company president, Mr. Buster Alan, requesting payment. Of course you do not want to antagonize Mr. Alan, because the company has been a client for several years and you value the business relationship.

Write the letter to Mr. Alan asking him to pay the bill.

Exercise 7-4 (all levels)

You are preparing the federal income tax returns for Mr. and Mrs. John Lapp and find you need some additional information: receipts for contributions to their church, the name of their youngest child, and the name of the day care center where the child is enrolled.

Write a letter to Mr. and Mrs. Lapp requesting this information.

Exercise 7-5 (all levels)

Schaeffer Art Supply has poor internal control over its cash transactions. Recently Mr. G. M. Schaeffer, the owner, has suspected the cashier of stealing. Details of the business's cash position at September 30 follow.

1. The Cash account shows a balance of $19,502. This amount includes a September 30 deposit of $3,794 that does not appear on the September 30 bank statement.
2. The September 30 bank statement shows a balance of $17,924. The bank statement lists a $200 credit for a bank collection, an $8 debit for the service charge, and a $36 debit for an NSF check. The Schaeffer accountant has not recorded any of these items on the books.
3. At September 30 the following checks are outstanding:

CHECK NO.	AMOUNT
154	$116
256	150
278	253
291	190
292	206
293	145

4. The cashier handles all incoming cash and makes the bank deposits. He also reconciles the monthly bank statement. His September 30 reconciliation follows.

Balance per books, September 30			$19,502
Add: Outstanding checks			2,060
Bank collection.............................			200
			21,762
Less: Deposits in transit		$3,794	
Service charge		8	
NSF check		36	3,838
Balance per bank, September 30			$17,924

Mr. Shaeffer has requested that you determine whether the cashier has stolen cash from the business and, if so, how much. Mr. Schaeffer also asks you to identify how the cashier has attempted to conceal the theft. To make this determination, you perform your own bank reconciliation. There are no bank or book errors. Mr. Schaeffer also asks you to evaluate the internal controls and to recommend any changes needed to improve them.[9]

Write a letter to Mr. Schaeffer that addresses his concerns.

Exercise 7-6 (Intermediate)

One morning J. Worthington Pocketmoney stormed into the offices of Apple, Altos, and Monroe, his certified public accountants. Without waiting for the receptionist to announce his arrival, he entered the office of Samuel Andrews, the partner in charge of auditing Mr. Pocketmoney's home appliance store. As usual, Mr. Andrews listened politely and calmly to the monologue delivered by Mr. Pocketmoney. An edited version follows.

This morning at my breakfast club I spoke with my competitor, F. Scott Wurlitzer. He boasted that his accountant had saved him $19,000 in income taxes last year by recommending a switch from the FIFO to the LIFO inventory flow assumption.

If he can do that, why can't I? And why haven't you discussed this gimmick with me? I don't expect to rely on Wurlitzer for financial advice; I pay you for that.

After Pocketmoney's departure, Mr. Andrews calls you, a new staff account-ant, into his office. He expresses regret at not having mentioned to Pocketmoney the possibility of a change in accounting method. However, he also advises you that Pocketmoney needs new capital in his business and is trying to interest another local businessperson in becoming a limited partner. Thus a decline in reported income could be detrimental to Mr. Pocketmoney's plans.

Mr. Andrews asks you to draft a letter to Mr. Pocketmoney. The letter should provide a balanced discussion of the advantages and disadvantages of shifting from FIFO to LIFO, with particular reference to Mr. Pocketmoney's specific situation. Even though Andrews would like to provide some justification for his firm's failure to mention the possibility of a change, he cautions you to be reasonably objective and consider accounting theory.[10]

Exercise 7-7 (Intermediate)

Your client, I. Seemdim, has written a letter to you. He is concerned that he has just received an offer to purchase his business for $1,000,000 more than the net carrying value of the assets on the most recent balance sheet audited by you. He is not interested in selling the business, but is now convinced that the value of his business is not properly reflected in the recently certified financial statements. He has been told by the prospective purchaser that the fair market value of the net separately identifiable assets is about $700,000 more than is shown in the balance sheet and that in addition there is at least $300,000 in goodwill that the would-be purchaser is willing to pay for.

Write a letter to your client explaining why the figures in the balance sheet should not be changed. Include an explanation of what goodwill is and why even though it may exist for his company it should not appear on the balance sheet. You may assume your client is an astute businessman but with no background in accounting.[11]

Exercise 7-8 (Intermediate)

Carla Bryant wishes to invest in an annuity for her son, Charles, who is ten years old. She wants the annuity to pay exactly $10,000 a year for five years, beginning when Charles turns 21. She wants to know how much money she will have to invest now, assuming the money will earn interest, compounded annually, of 8 percent.

Write a letter to Ms. Bryant explaining annuities and the amount she would need to invest now to set up the plan she has in mind.

Execise 7-9 (Intermediate)

At the beginning of the year, Patrick Company acquired a computer to be used in its operations. The computer was delivered by the supplier, installed by the owner, Rob Patrick, and placed into operation. The estimated useful life of the computer is five years, and its estimated residual (salvage) value is significant.

During the year, Mr. Patrick received cash in exchange for an automobile that was purchased in a prior year.

Required:

- What costs should Mr. Patrick capitalize for the computer?
- How should Mr. Patrick account for and report the disposal of the automobile?

Write a letter to Mr. Patrick in which you answer these questions.[12]

Exercise 7-10 (Intermediate)

You are a senior staff accountant with the firm of Taxum and Howe in Oberlin, Ohio. Your new client, Mr. Grabmore Gusto, would like your advice. Mr. Gusto is concerned about having audited financial statements for the first time this year.

To begin operations three years ago, Mr. Gusto invested $300,000 of his own money (his life savings) and borrowed $200,000 from Oberlin Bank and Trust. The loan carries a 10 percent interest rate and has a term of ten years from the date of issuance. Mr. Gusto set up a sinking fund immediately and has made monthly deposits to assure timely payments of interest and principal. Because of the success of his business, Mr. Gusto has been able to deposit enough money in three years to cover interest for the remaining seven years as well as the principal.

Mr. Gusto has recently developed a plan to expand his business, but needs to borrow about $500,000 to implement the plan. He is concerned, however, that Oberlin Bank and Trust will not grant him a new loan because of the existence of the original loan.

A business acquaintance, Mr. Suds, has suggested that because Mr. Gusto has deposited enough money in the sinking fund to cover principal and interest, he can simply eliminate both the sinking fund assets and the liability from his balance sheet. Mr. Suds referred to the elimination as debt defeasance.

Mr. Gusto is afraid that such an elimination or cancellation would not be in accordance with GAAP and would therefore result in a qualified audit opinion.

Write Mr. Gusto a letter explaining debt defeasance, including in your discussion a recommendation as to the conformity (or lack thereof) with GAAP. He has researched the problem and is somewhat familiar with various applications and accounting treatments of defeasance.[13]

Exercise 7-11 (Intermediate)

Suppose you were the CPA to whom the letter in Figure 7-6 was written. Write a letter in reply.[14]

KEN-L-PRODUCTS, INC.

749 E. Peartree St.

Manhattan, Kansas 66502

                                        May 1, 1992

Ellen Acker, CPA
331 J.M. Tull Street
Manhattan, KS 66502

Dear Ms. Acker:

As you well know, it is becoming impossible to conduct business without the
constant threat of litigation. This year our company is faced with several
lawsuits. We are unsure how these suits should be treated in our financial
statements and would like clarification before you audit us this year.

Would you please specify the disclosure requirements for the following circumstances:

(1) Several show dog owners have filed a class-action suit concerning
     the product "Shampoodle." The plaintiffs claim that severe hair
     loss has occurred as a result of product use. The suit is for a
     total of $2 million. However, our attorneys claim that it is
     probable that will have to pay only between $500,000 and $1 million.

(2) For quite sometime we have been producing a dog food called
     "Ken-L-Burgers." Recently we changed the formula and advertised
     the product as "better tasting." A consumer group known as "Spokes-
     man for Dogs" has filed suit claiming that humans must actually eat
     the product in order to make the claim of better taste. Our lawyers
     say that the chance of losing this suit is remote. The suit is for
     $6 million.

(3) One of our workers lost a finger in the "Ken-L-Burger" machine.
     Our attorneys believe that we will probably lose this suit but are
     unsure about the amount.

(4) My brother's company, House of Cats, is being sued for $4 million.
     His lawyers say that it is not likely that he will lose. How-
     ever, Ken-L-Products, Inc., has guaranteed a debt he owes to a bank.
     If he loses, he will not be able to pay the bank.

FIGURE 7-6   A Letter from a Client. (Exercise 7-11.)

Ellen Acker
May 1, 1992
Page 2

    (5) A grain company sold us several tons of spoiled grain used as
         filler in our products. Since the company will not reimburse
         us for the spoilage, we have sued for $2 million. Our attorneys
         say we will probably win the case.

    (6) We aired several commercials that claimed Wayne Newton's dog uses
         our products. Mr. Newton told us that his dog hates our products
         and that if we show the commercials again he will probably sue us.

If each of these items is material, should we show them on the financial statements?

Thank you for your help on these disclosures.

Sincerely,

Ken L Price

Ken L. Price

FIGURE 7-6   Continued

Exercise 7-12 (Auditing)

Write an engagement letter in which you agree to review the financial statements of Howard Fabricators, Inc. You may mention other services that you agree to provide.

Exercise 7-13 (Auditing)

One of your audit clients is Brown Manufacturing, which is owned by Charles Brown. Although your client has not discussed the problem with you, you have concluded that the business is in dire need of additional liquid funds. You have noted that payables are being liquidated well after discount dates have expired and that most equipment is being leased, rather than being purchased as is customary in most businesses of this type. The problem is being aggravated by a continued increase in volume, which has necessitated carrying larger inventories and receivables and leasing additional equipment at rates well in excess of normal depreciation charges and interest. The owner of the business has already invested all his available liquid funds in the business.[15]

Write a letter to Mr. Brown, suggesting ways he could improve the liquidity of his business.

Exercise 7-14 (Auditing)

A competent auditor has done a conscientious job of auditing Brown Corporation, but because of a clever fraud by management, a material error is included in the financial statements. The irregularity, which is an overstatement of inventory, took place over several years, and it covered up the fact that the company's financial position was rapidly declining. The fraud was accidentally discovered in the lastest audit by an unusually capable audit senior, and the SEC was immediately informed. Subsequent investigation indicated Brown Corporation was actually near bankruptcy, and the value of the stock dropped from $26 per share to $1 in less than one month. Among the losing stockholders were pension funds, university endowment funds, retired couples, and widows. The individuals responsible for perpetrating the fraud were also bankrupt.

After making an extensive investigation of the audit performance in previous years, the SEC was satisfied that the auditor had done a high-quality audit and had followed generally accepted auditing standards in every respect. The commission concluded that it would be unreasonable to expect auditors to uncover this type of fraud.

One of your clients, Elizabeth Adams, is a stockholder in Brown Corporation. She has written you to express her dismay about the decline in value of her stock. She also wants to know who should bear the loss of the management fraud. Mrs. Adams is an intelligent, well-educated person but she knows very little about business or accounting.

Write a letter to Mrs. Adams that will address her concerns.[16]

Exercise 7-15 (Cost)

Consider the following data of the Laimon Company for the year 19__1:

Sandpaper	$ 2,000	Depreciation—equipment	$ 40,000
Material handling	40,000	Factory rent	50,000
Lubricants and coolants	5,000	Property taxes on equipment	4,000
Overtime premium	20,000	Fire insurance on equipment	3,000
Idle time	10,000	Direct materials purchased	460,000
Miscellaneous indirect labor	40,000	Direct materials, 12/31/__1	50,000
Direct labor	300,000	Sales	1,260,000
Direct materials, 12/31/__	40,000	Sales commissions	60,000
Finished goods, 12/31/__1	150,000	Sales salaries	100,000
Finished goods, 12/31/__0	100,000	Shipping expenses	70,000
Work in process, 12/31/__0	10,000	Administrative expenses	100,000
Work in process, 12/31/__1	14,000		

a. Suppose that both the direct-material and rent costs were related to the manufacturing of the equivalent of 900,000 units. What is the average unit cost for the direct materials assigned to those units? What is the average cost of the factory rent? Assume that the rent is a fixed cost.

b. Repeat the computation in requirement a for direct materials and factory rent, assuming that the costs are being predicted for the manufacturing of the equivalent of 1,000,000 units next year. Assume that the implied cost behavior patterns persist.

As a management consultant, explain concisely in a letter to the president why the unit costs for direct materials and rent differed in requirements a and b.[17]

Exercise 7-16
(Advanced Managerial or
Financial)

Assume one of the following situations:

1. You are a senior member of the auditing staff of a medium-sized manufacturing corporation.

OR

2. You are a partner of a regional accounting firm.

Write a letter to the Financial Accounting Standards Board in response to a recent FASB Exposure Draft.

Exercise 7-17
(Accounting Information
Systems)

Parker's Shoe Store has been owned and managed by a very conservative individual who is intimidated by computers. The money from cash sales is kept in an old-fashioned cash register, and clerks keep track of the shoes sold by recording pertinent information (brand, style number, price, and size) on a yellow legal pad.

The owner of the store is planning to retire soon and his daughter, Sue Parker, will then be the full-time manager. She believes a computer system could help her run the store more efficiently, and she hires you to evaluate the store's needs and explain how a computer system could help her manage the business.

Write a letter to Ms. Parker explaining the benefits to the store of a computer system, as well as its limitations. Remember that while she is open-minded about the usefulness of computers, she knows very little about them.

Exercise 7-18
(Accounting Information
Systems)

One of your clients, a small service business with ten office employees, plans to purchase a database package for use with the office's personal computers.

Select two database packages and evaluate them for your client's needs. Consider the advantages and disadvantages of both packages, including the ease with which the staff will be able to learn the new system. You should consider basic features of the database package as well as advanced functions.

Write your evaluation in the form of a letter to the company's president, Heather Owen.

Exercise 7-19
(Tax)

Elaine Harrison was divorced in 1991. Her unmarried daughter lived in her home for the entire year. It cost $6,000 to maintain her home in 1990, of which her former husband contributed $2,000 through support payments. Her former husband also provides more than half of their daughter's total support and claims her as a dependent under a written agreement with his ex-wife. What is Mrs. Harrison's correct filing status for the year?[18]

Write a letter to Mrs. Harrison in which you explain the answer to this question.

NOTES

1. Ray M. Sommerfeld, G. Fred Streuling, Robert L. Gardner, and Dave N. Stewart, *Tax Research Techniques,* 3rd ed., Revised (New York: American Institute of Certified Public Accountants, 1989), pp. 163–64. This source provides additional information on other letters that tax accountants may write, such as tax protest letters and requests for rulings.
2. W. Peter Van Son, Dan M. Guy, and J. Frank Betts, "Engagement Letters: What Practice Shows," *Journal of Accountancy,* 152, no. 6 (June 1982), p. 76.
3. Robert T. Lanz and S. Thomas Moser, "Improving Management Letters," *Journal of Accountancy,* 149, no. 3 (March 1980), pp. 39–42.

4. Ibid., p. 42.

5. Ibid., pp. 41–42.

6. Sommerfeld, et al. pp. 164–65.

7. Adapted from Sommerfeld, et al., pp. 184–86.

8. Adapted from William A. Raebe, Gerald E. Whittenburg, and John C. Bost, *West's Federal Tax Research* (St. Paul: West Publishing Company, 1987), p. 259.

9. Adapted from Charles T. Horngren and Walter T. Harrison, *Accounting* (Englewood Cliffs, N.J.: Prentice Hall, Inc., 1989), p. 306. Reprinted by permission.

10. Randolph A. Shockley, "Writing Assignment for Intermediate Accounting" (unpublished class assignment, University of Georgia, 1982).

11. Gordon S. May, "Writing Assignment for Intermediate Accounting" (unpublished class assignment, University of Georgia, 1990).

12. Adapted from American Institute of Certified Public Accountants, *Uniform CPA Exam: Questions and Unofficial Answers,* November 1988 (New York: AICPA, 1989), p. 54.

13. George Peek, "Writing Assignment for Intermediate Accounting" (unpublished class assignment, University of Georgia, 1986).

14. William R. Pasewark, "Writing Assignment for Intermediate Accounting" (unpublished class assignment, University of Georgia, 1987).

15. Adapted from Howard F. Stettler, *Auditing Principles: A Systems-Based Approach* (Englewood Cliffs, N.J.: Prentice-Hall, Inc., ©1982), pp. 667–68. Reprinted by permission.

16. Adapted from Alvin A. Arens and James K. Loebbecke, *Auditing: An Integrated Approach,* 4th ed. (Englewood Cliffs, N.J.: Prentice Hall, Inc., 1988), p. 155. Reprinted by permission.

17. Adapted from Charles T. Horngren and George Foster, *Cost Accounting: A Managerial Emphasis,* 6th ed. (Englewood Cliffs, N.J.: Prentice Hall, Inc., 1987), p. 37. Reprinted by permission.

18. Adapted from Prentice Hall, *1988 Federal Tax Course* (Englewood Cliffs, N.J.: Prentice-Hall, Inc., ©1987), p. 81. Reprinted by permission.

8

MEMOS

Memos, also called memoranda or memorandums, are used for communication within an organization—between departments, for example, or between supervisor and staff. Memos may be of any length, from one sentence to several pages. They may be less formal than letters written to people outside the organization, but well-written memos have the same qualities as good letters: coherence, clarity, conciseness, and courtesy—all the techniques of the "you attitude."

This chapter will first discuss some of the general characteristics of effective memos. Then we will look at two special kinds of memos that accountants often write: memos to clients' files and memos that are part of working papers.

MEMOS: SOME BASIC PRINCIPLES

Frequently memos are quite short—from one sentence, perhaps, to several paragraphs. Figure 8-1 is an example. Notice the heading of the memo: the date, the person or persons addressed, the writer, and the subject. Frequently the writer's initials replace a formal signature.

Sometimes memos may be much longer than the one in Figure 8-1; in fact, they may be used for short reports. For longer memos, organization and structure are more complicated, so you will need to think of writing the memo in terms of the writing process discussed in Chapter 2. For example, you will need to spend

```
                              MEMO



To:          All Employees

From:        John Moore  𝒴ⁱⁿ

Subject:     Ruth Morgan's Retirement Party

Date:        June 5, 1992


     As many of you know, Ruth Morgan will be retiring next month after

35 years on our accounting staff.

     We are planning a party in Ruth's honor on Wednesday, July 1.  The

party will be at the Town Club from 5:00 PM to 7:00 PM.

     We hope everyone will be present to show Ruth our appreciation and

best wishes.  Please let me know by June 23 if you and your spouse or

friend will be able to attend.
```

FIGURE 8-1 A Short Memo.

some time planning your memo: analyzing its purpose, considering the needs and interests of your readers, and finally organizing the material to be covered into a good outline. Once you have planned the memo, you can then draft and revise it using the techniques covered in Chapters 2–6.

The Parts of a Memo:
Organizing for Coherence

As with most kinds of writing, a memo is organized into an introduction, a body, and a conclusion. Summary sentences are used throughout the memo to make it more coherent.

Introduction.   Most introductions are one paragraph long, although for a longer memo the introduction may be two or three short paragraphs. The introduction should identify what the memo is about and why it was written. If the memo will discuss more than one topic or be divided into several subtopics, the introduction should identify all the most important issues to be covered. For example, the introduction might contain a sentence such as the following to indicate the memo's contents:

This memo will explain how to account for patents, copyrights, and trademarks.

An introduction should also identify the main ideas and/or recommendations of your memo. Sometimes the main idea can be summarized in one or two sentences, but for longer memos, you may need an entire paragraph. If the summary of your main ideas is longer than a paragraph, it's often better to put it in a separate section immediately following the introduction. This section would have a heading such as "Summary" or "Recommendations."

Body.   The body of the memo is divided into sections, each with a heading that describes the contents of that section. Remember to begin by summarizing the main idea of the section.

A section may have one or many paragraphs. Paragraphs should usually be no more than four or five sentences long, and each should begin with a topic sentence.

Conclusion.   Memos often end with a conclusion, which may be very brief:

Let me know if you have any further questions about these procedures.

A conclusion such as this one brings the memo to a close, and ends in a courteous, helpful tone. Here's a word of caution, though, about conclusions like the one just given: be careful not to end all your memos with the same sentence (or some slightly altered variation). The conclusion should be a *meaningful* addition to the memo, not just an empty string of words added out of habit. The sample memos in this chapter show several different kinds of conclusions; all are appropriate to the content of the memo.

One misconception that some people have about conclusions is that they should always repeat the memo's main ideas. For short memos, this repetition is usually not necessary, although for memos longer than about three or four pages such an ending summary may be helpful.

Whatever the length of the memo, however, the conclusion is a good place to tell your readers what you want them to do, or what you will do, to follow up on the ideas discussed in the memo. The memo in Figure 8-1 has such a conclusion.

Concise, Clear, Readable Memos: Style and Tone

Memos should, of course, be as concise as possible: no unnecessary repetitions or digressions and no wordiness. They should be written in a clear, direct style, so that readers find them interesting and informative. Finally, memos should be flawless in grammar and mechanics.

Memos can vary considerably in tone, depending on what they are about and how they will be circulated. Some memos, such as the one in Figure 8-1, are quite informal. For these memos, a conversational, personal tone is appropriate.

Other memos are more formal and may in fact serve as short reports. Some memos, such as those reporting the results of research or work performed, may become part of the permanent records in a client's file. These memos are usually written with a more impersonal, formal tone. But whether formal or informal, all memos should be written in a vigorous, readable style.

Formats

Memos can be written in a variety of formats, as the examples in this chapter show. The memo in Figure 8-2 is typical of the format used in many organizations. Notice especially how the headings and set-off list make this memo attractive and easy to read.

Some organizations prefer another format that has become customary within the organization. You should, of course, prepare your memos according to your employer's expectations. The example in Figure 8-3 illustrates a format that some CPA firms prefer when the memos are part of an audit file.

SAMPLE MEMOS

The memo shown in Figure 8-2 was written in response to the hypothetical situation described below.

Situation:
Fred Lee is the proprietor of the firm for which you work. Mr. Lee wants to acquire
(continued on p. 135.)

MEMORANDUM   August 16, 1992

TO: FRED LEE

FROM: PETE WARDLAW

SUBJECT: PURCHASING DCL BROADCASTING

This memo is in response to your questions concerning the purchase of
DCL Broadcasting. The memo will first explain goodwill and then discuss
how to determine its cost. I suggest computing the value of goodwill to help
determine DCL's maximum value. Thus, you would have a dollar amount to help
you determine how much you want to offer for the company.

What Is Goodwill?

Goodwill is an intangible asset made up of items that may contribute
to the value and earning power of a company. Some possible items that may
make up goodwill for DCL Broadcasting are :

  1) High ratings

  2) Access to the most popular shows and movies

  3) Good managerial staff

  4) A large number of advertisers

These items increase the earnings of DCL Broadcasting, but they are not
listed on DCL's balance sheet. However, the amount of DCL's goodwill should
be included in the purchase price of the business.

Determining the Cost of Goodwill

Excess cost over net assets and excess earnings are two ways to

FIGURE 8-2 A Memo.

Fred Lee

August 16, 1992

Page 2

determine the cost of goodwill. The first method computes goodwill by subtracting the purchase price from the fair market value of DCL Broadcasting's net assets. The second method uses DCL's past earnings and the normal earnings of the broadcasting industry to compute estimated excess earnings of DCL Broadcasting. Both methods will estimate goodwill for DCL; however, I suggest using the excess earnings method because it will allow you to see an estimated rate of return on your investment.

Let me know if you have any further questions about goodwill or the DCL acquisition.

FIGURE 8-2 Continued

April 1, 1992

TO: Files
FROM: Tom Partner
SUBJECT: Potential acquisition by American Rock & Sand, Inc. of
          Pahrump Ready Mix, Inc.

Today, Ron Jones, financial vice-president of American Rock & Sand, Inc.
(ARS), called to request information concerning the tax consequences of a proposed acquisition of Pahrump Ready Mix, Inc. (PRM). ARS is a Utah corporation
(organized on October 1, 1962) licensed as a general contractor and specializes
in road and highway construction. ARS employs the accrual method of accounting
and uses a calendar year end as the basis for maintaining its books. ARS's
authorized capital consists of 1,000 shares of voting common stock owned principally by the Jones family.

PRM, the target corporation, is a Utah Corporation organized on June 1,
1970. PRM is engaged in the business of making and delivering concrete. PRM
employs the accrual method of accounting and uses a calendar year end as the
basis for maintaining its books. PRM's authorized capital consists of 5,000
shares of voting common stock owned principally by the Smith family.

ARS has approached PRM about the possibility of acquiring the assets of
PRM. PRM has expressed some preliminary interest if the deal can be structured
so that the Smith family is not taxed on the initial sale of PRM. The Smith
family has stated that they would consider receiving ARS stock as long as the
stock will provide them with an annual income.

Due to a shortage of cash, ARS would like to accomplish the acquisition
without the use of cash. Also, the Jones family has stated strenuously that
they are not interested in giving up any voting power in ARS to the Smith
family. John Jones has requested that we develop, if possible, a proposal
of how ARS can structure the transaction to satisfy the requests of both ARS
and PRM. Mr. Jones has requested that we present at their May 1, 1992, ARS
board meeting our proposal for the acquisition of PRM. If we need further
information, we are to contact Mr. Jones directly.

FIGURE 8-3   A Memo to a Client's File.

a broadcasting business. The business he wants to acquire, DCL Broadcasting, is insisting that Fred pay not only for the identifiable net assets of the business, but also for something called "goodwill." Fred says to you: "What is this goodwill stuff? Should I pay for it or not? If I should pay for it, how much should I pay?"[1]

Study the memo in Figure 8-2[2] to see how it illustrates the principles of memo writing already discussed. Do you think Mr. Lee will be pleased with the memo? Why or why not?

Memos to Clients' Files

Accountants often record information about a client's situation in a memo that is placed in the client's file for later reference. Other members of the staff may refer to the information recorded in these memos months or even years later, so the information must be recorded clearly, accurately, and correctly.

For example, a client may write or call an accounting firm about a tax question. The person receiving the letter or handling the call will then write a memo to record the pertinent facts of the client's situation. Later, another member of the staff can research the question. The researcher will need adequate information to identify the issues, locate appropriate literature, and solve the client's problem.[3]*

A sample memo written for a client's file appears in Figure 8-3.[4]**

Memos as Part of Working Papers

When accountants prepare working papers as part of their work on a case, they usually include memos summarizing the work they have performed, what they have observed, and the conclusions they have reached. In an audit, for example, the audit staff members prepare memos describing each major area of the audit. Then a supervisor, perhaps the auditor in charge or the engagement partner, will often prepare a summary or review memo that includes comments on the entire audit process.

These memos must be clear, accurate, and complete. Other members of the firm, or lawyers on either side of a court case who review the working papers later, may need to know exactly what procedures the auditors performed. Thus, the memos should be written in a direct, active style: "I [the person writing the memo] performed a cash receipts walk-through on May 31, 1992. I used admission ticket #51065 for the test."

The memo in Figure 8-4 was written to record an inventory observation.[5] This memo has a different organization and format from the sample memos given earlier in the chapter. Yet it illustrates the three qualities essential for effective writing: coherence, conciseness, and clarity. What specific techniques make this memo effective?

---

*Copyright © 1989 by the American Institute of Certified Public Accountants, Inc.
**Copyright © 1989 by the American Institute of Certified Public Accountants, Inc.

Highlight Company
Inventory Observation Memorandum—Wayne Plant A
12/31/91

1. Observing clients' inventory taking. Four members of our audit staff
    arrived at the Wayne plant at 7:40 A.M. on 12/31/91 for the inventory
    observation. All manufacturing and shipping operations had been shut
    down for the day. All materials had been neatly arranged, labeled and
    separated by type.

    Two teams of audit staff members were assigned to different parts of
    the plant. Each team observed the care with which the client's personnel
    made the inventory counts and the control being exercised over the in-
    ventory count sheets. In every case, it appeared that the client's inven-
    tory instructions were being followed in a systematic and conscientious
    manner.

2. Making test counts. Each team made numerous test counts, which were
    recorded in our work papers (see F-2). The test counts covered approxi-
    mately 22 percent of the inventory value and confirmed the accuracy of
    the client's counts.

3. Identifying obsolete and damaged goods. Each team made inquiries con-
    cerning obsolete, damaged, or slow-moving items. Based on our observations
    and inquiries, we have no reason to believe that any obsolete or damaged
    materials remained in inventory. We identified certain slow-moving items,
    portions of which on further investigation were excluded from the inventory
    (see F-4).

4. Observing cutoff controls. We observed that receiving reports were pre-
    pared on all goods received on the inventory date and recorded the number
    of the last receiving report prepared. No goods were shipped on 12/31.
    We recorded the number of the last shipping document used on 12/30. These
    numbers were subsequently used in our purchases and sales cutoff tests
    (see F-6 and F-7).

5. Conclusions. Based on our observation of the procedures followed by the
    client, it is my opinion that an accurate count was made of all goods
    on hand at 12/31/91 and that all obsolete, damaged, or slow-moving items
    were appropriately identified.

                                                        Carl Good
                                                        C.G.

FIGURE 8-4 A Memo as Part of Working Papers.

When your job requires you to write a memo, remember the techniques of effective writing stressed throughout this book. *Coherent* memos are logically organized and easy to follow; *concise* memos cover essential information in as few words as possible; and *clear* memos are precise, readable, and grammatically correct.

EXERCISES

Exercise 8-1
(All Levels)

You work in the accounting department of Gigantic Corporation. The company's Chief Executive Officer, Mary Sanders, has asked you to be in charge of your department's fund raising for the United Way campaign.

Write a memo to your coworkers asking them to contribute to this year's campaign. The memo will accompany a pledge card that they may fill in and sign. Make the memo persuasive, and add any details you think would make the memo effective.

Exercise 8-2
(All Levels)

You are newly hired as an accountant for the O-Y-Me Corporation, which is a small service business currently using the cash basis of accounting. The president of your company, Mr. Now U. Donit, has requested that you write a memo to him explaining what the accrual basis of accounting is, how it differs from the cash basis, and why O-Y-Me should switch from the cash basis to the accrual basis.[6]

Exercise 8-3
(All Levels)

You are the controller of Carr Corporation. One morning you receive the memo in Figure 8-5 from the president of your company, Mr. W. R. Pasewark. Write a memo in response to the president's questions.[7]

Exercise 8-4
(All Levels)

You are a loan officer at Gotham City National Bank. The proprietors of two businesses, Butler Department Store and Susan Nielsen Home Decorators, have sought business loans from you. To decide whether to make the loans, you have requested their balance sheets, which are shown in Figure 8-6. Based solely on these balance sheets, which entity would you be more comfortable loaning money to? Explain fully, citing specific items and amounts from the balance sheets. Write your answer in the form of a memo to the bank's Vice President, Edward Barth.[8]

CARR CORPORATION

OFFICE MEMO

To: I.N. Dunne, Controller

From: W.R. Pasewark, President

Date: June 26, 1992

Subject: Who sets the rules for accounting?

As you know, this will be the first year that our company has issued
financial statements. I am particularly concerned about what rules we must
follow in preparing our financial statements to accomodate our external
auditors.

Recently, I examined the audited financial statements of a company similar
to ours. The auditor's opinion section mentioned that the financial statements
were prepared in accordance with "generally accepted accounting principles."
I suspect that these are the rules that we must follow when preparing our own
financial statements.

Would you please help me by answering the following questions concerning
generally accepted accounting principles:

1.   Who determines generally accepted accounting principles?
2.   If we violate these rules, will we be breaking the law?
3.   If these rules are not law, why must we follow them?

FIGURE 8-5   Memo for Exercise 8-3.

Butler Department Store
Balance Sheet
August 31, 19X4

Assets		Liabilities	
Cash	$ 1,000	Accounts payable	$ 12,000
Accounts receivable	14,000	Note payable	18,000
Merchandise inventory	85,000	Total liabilities	30,000
Store supplies	500		
Furniture and fixtures	9,000	Owner's Equity	
Building	90,000		
Land	14,000	Roy Butler, capital	183,500
Total assets	$213,500	Total liabilities and owner's equity	$213,500

Susan Nielsen Home Decorators
Balance Sheet
August 31, 19X4

Assets		Liabilities	
Cash	$11,000	Accounts payable	$ 3,000
Accounts receivable	4,000	Note payable	18,000
Office supplies	1,000	Total liabilities	21,000
Office furniture	6,000		
Land	19,000	Owner's Equity	
		Susan Nielsen, capital	20,000
Total asssets	$41,000	Total liabilities and owner's equity	$41,000

FIGURE 8-6   For Exercise 8-4.

Exercise 8-5
(Intermediate)

You are the controller of the Red Mesa Ranch and are preparing the ranch's financial statements for the year. You requested information from the cattle manager, Tuf Cowan, about the value of the ranch's livestock assets. Mr. Cowan sent you the memo in Figure 8-7, which asks you some questions about how to classify the livestock. Write a memo to answer Mr. Cowan's questions.[9]

Exercise 8-6
(Intermediate)

You are the CPA for Ms. Ima Astute, who owns a small business. Ms. Astute is considering the purchase of a competing business. The sum of the fair market values of the separately identifiable assets of the business she may purchase is $350,000. Ms. Astute determined this by having an appraisal made before making

RED MESA RANCH

OFFICE MEMO

To: Ian Greenberg, Controller

From: Tuf Cowan, Cattle Manager

Date: June 28, 1992

Subject: Classification of livestock on the balance sheet

       I have received your request to value our livestock assets for the balance
sheet for the year ending June 30, 1991. Based on available commodity prices,
I can easily determine the dollar value of the livestock. However, I am unable
to determine whether the following livestock categories should be shown as
current items (inventory) or as long-term items:

1. Bulls--kept for breeding purposes; average useful life of ten years.

2. Steers--held for approximately 15 months from birth, then sold for
    slaughter.

3. Heifers--most kept for breeding purposes; average useful life of five years,
    then sold for slaughter.

5. Calves--less than one year old, certain percentage sold as veal, others
    used for breeding or grazed and sold later for slaughter.

       Would you please assist me by specifying how I should classify each of
these categories?

FIGURE 8-7 Memo for Exercise 8-5.

an offer. The offer she made was equal to this amount, i.e., $350,000. The owner of the business she wants to purchase has declined the offer and indicated he thinks his business is worth at least $400,000 considering the goodwill that exists. Ms. Astute cannot understand how the business can be worth more than $350,000 considering this was the amount of the appraisal.

Write a letter to Ms. Astute explaining what goodwill is, why it may exist for the business she wants to purchase, how she may determine what to pay for it, and the effects on future financial statements she may expect.[10]

Exercise 8-7
(Intermediate)

Skinner Company has the following contingencies:

- Potential costs due to the discovery of a possible defect related to one of its products. These costs are probable and can be reasonably estimated.
- A potential claim for damages to be received from a lawsuit filed this year against another company. It is probable that proceeds from the claim will be received by Skinner next year.
- Potential costs due to a promotion campaign whereby a cash refund is sent to customers when coupons are redeemed. Skinner estimated, based on past experience, that 70 percent of the coupons would be redeemed. Forty percent of the coupons were actually redeemed and the cash refunds sent this year. The remaining 30 percent of the coupons are expected to be redeemed next year.

Required:
a. How should Skinner report the potential costs due to the discovery of a possible product defect? Why?
b. How should Skinner report this year the potential claim for damages that may be received next year? Why?
c. This year, how should Skinner account for the potential costs and obligations due to the promotion campaign?

You are a staff accountant at Skinner Company. Write your answer in the form of a memo to the company's controller, Daniel Gordon.[11]

Exercise 8-8
(Intermediate)

You have been hired as a special assistant to Sam Jones, the president of Bulldog Sales Company. Mr. Jones has little formal education but is very astute about business matters and is an especially good salesperson. He calls you in and says, "Bulldog Sales Company is in the nice position of having excess cash on hand. I am considering investing that cash in some bonds issued five years ago by Red and Black Company, but I see in the *Wall Street Journal* that those bonds are selling at only 60 percent of their maturity value. Does that mean they are especially risky? Assuming I do make this investment, what are the accounting implications?''

Write a memo answering Mr. Jones's questions.[12]

Exercise 8-9
(Intermediate)

As a member of the technical staff of your CPA firm, you receive a request from a member of the audit staff for assistance in determining how to account for a large inventory of one of your clients. The company involved is a manufacturing firm that makes custom-designed machine parts. There are only two other companies in the country with the technology to produce these parts. Your client's firm is the largest of the three. Management has built a reputation not only for the quality of its products but also for customer service. One of the most successful policies it follows is always to manufacture a larger quantity of a part than a customer orders. The extra parts are kept in inventory so that if the customer later has an emergency need for the part, several may be shipped in a matter of two or three hours. The customers don't know that extra parts are being inventoried and therefore think that your client stops all other production to respond to the emergency. This greatly impresses customers and because of this, business has grown tremendously.

The problem is that any given customer will rarely, if ever, use this service. As a consequence, your client has built a huge inventory of production overruns, and only a small indeterminable amount of it is likely to be used. Your client does not show the inventory on the balance sheet because of its practice to expense the extra cost of production overruns as part of the cost of the production sold. A very large warehouse devoted entirely to this inventory is shown on the balance sheet, however, and is depreciated assuming a 20-year life.

Write a memo to Mr. Y. Doit of the audit staff stating your position on how to account for this inventory; deal with any other ramifications you may perceive. Your position should be formed after a *thorough* research of GAAP.[13]

Exercise 8-10
(Intermediate)

Milton Corporation entered into a lease arrangement with James Leasing Corporation for a certain machine. James's primary business is leasing and it is not a manufacturer or dealer. Milton will lease the machine for a period of three years, which is 50 percent of the machine's economic life. James will take possession of the machine at the end of the initial three-year lease and lease it to another, smaller company that does not need the most current version of the machine. Milton does not guarantee any residual value for the machine and will not purchase the machine at the end of the lease term.

Milton's incremental borrowing rate is 10 percent and the implicit rate in the lease is 8½ percent. Milton has no way of knowing the implicit rate used by

James. Using either rate, the present value of the minimum lease payments is between 90 percent and 100 percent of the fair value of the machine at the date of the agreement.

Milton has agreed to pay all executory costs directly and no allowance for these costs is included in the lease payments.

James is reasonably certain that Milton will pay all lease payments, and, because Milton has agreed to pay all executory costs, there are no important uncertainties regarding costs to be incurred by James.

With respect to Milton (the lessee) answer the following:

1. What type of lease has been entered into? Explain the reason for your answer.
2. How should Milton compute the appropriate amount to be recorded for the lease or asset acquired?
3. What accounts will be created or affected by this transaction and how will the lease or asset and other costs related to the transaction be matched with earnings?
4. What disclosures must Milton make regarding this lease or asset?*

You are a staff accountant of the Milton Corporation. Write a memo to the controller, Helen Garcia, in which you answer these questions.

Exercise 8-11
(Intermediate or Auditing)

Cranium Products Company manufactures a variety of sports headgear, which it sells to hundreds of distributors and retailers.

A company "cash clerk" processes all cash received in the mail (mostly checks from customers on account). He opens the mail, sending to the accounting department all accompanying letters and remittance advices that show the amounts received from each customer or other source. The letters and remittance advices are used by the accounting department for appropriate entries in the accounts. The clerk sends the currency and checks to another employee, who makes daily bank deposits but has no access to the accounting records. The monthly bank statements are reconciled by the accounting department, which has no access to cash or checks.

The sales manager has the authority for granting credit to customers for sales returns and allowances, and the credit manager has the authority for deciding when uncollectible accounts should be written off. However, a recent audit revealed that the cash clerk had forged the signatures of the sales manager and the credit manager to some forms authorizing sales allowances and bad debt write-offs for certain accounts. These forms were then sent to the accounting department, which entered them on the books and routinely posted them to customers' accounts.

How could the cash clerk have used these forgeries to cover an embezzlement by him? Assume there was no collusion with other employees. Be specific.[14]

Write a memo to the president of Cranium in which you discuss this situation.

Exercise 8-12
(Auditing)

The firm for which you work, Temple and Temple, CPAs, is auditing the financial statements of Ford Lumber Yards, Inc., a privately held corporation with 300 employees and five stockholders, three of whom are active in management. Ford has been in business for many years, but has never had its financial statements audited. The partner in charge of the audit suspects that the substance of some of Ford's business transactions differs from their form because of the pervasiveness of related party relationships and transactions in the local building supplies industry.

Required:

Describe the audit procedures Temple should apply to identify related party relationships and transactions.[15]

Write your answer in the form of a memo to the staff accountants who will audit Ford.

Exercise 8-13
(Cost)

A supplier to an automobile manufacturer has the following conversation with the manufacturer's purchasing manager:

> SUPPLIER: You did not predict the heavy demands. To keep up with your unforeseen demands over the coming quarter, we will have to work six days per week instead of five. Therefore, I want a price increase in the amount of the overtime premium that I must pay.
>
> MANUFACTURER: You have already recouped your fixed costs, so you are enjoying a hefty contribution margin on the sixth day. So quit complaining!

Should the supplier get an increase in price?[16] Write your answer in the form of a memo to the president of the automobile manufacturing firm.

Exercise 8-14
(Cost or Intermediate)

The Thomas Company is in the process of developing a revolutionary new product. A new division of the company was formed to develop, manufacture, and market this new product. As of year end (December 31, 1992) the new product has not been manufactured for resale; however, a prototype unit was built and is in operation.

Throughout 1991 the new division incurred certain costs. These costs include design and engineering studies, prototype manufacturing costs, administrative expenses (including salaries of administrative personnel), and market research costs. In addition, approximately $500,000 in equipment (estimated useful life—10 years) was purchased for use in developing and manufacturing the new product. Approximately $200,000 of this equipment was built specifically for the design development of the new product; the remaining $300,000 of equipment was used to manufacture the preproduction prototype and will be used to manufacture the new product once it is in commercial production.

In accordance with Statement of Financial Accounting Standards No. 2, how should the various costs of Thomas described above be recorded on the financial statements for the year ended December 31, 1992?*

You are the controller of the Thomas Company. Write a memo to the president, Ruth Richards, in which you answer this question. Explain your answer in terms of SFAS No. 2.

Exercise 8–15
(Accounting Information Systems)

You are a new accountant on the staff of Walker Manufacturing. Walker has been on a manual accounting system, but now plans to convert to a computerized system.

The president of the company, Roland Walker, knows that there are several methods a company can use to convert from a manual to an automated system, but he does not know which method would be better for his company.

Write a memo to the president in which you compare the four methods of conversion, and recommend the best one for Walker Manufacturing.

Exercise 8–16
(Accounting Information Systems)

For many CPA firms, in-house tax preparation gives higher profitability and increased control. It may also lead to staff and client frustration if procedural nightmares or equipment inadequacies interfere with return preparation. A rule of thumb is that a firm preparing more than 200 returns a year could be more profitable with in-house rather than service bureau tax return preparation. This informal guide may not apply, however, in all cases.

Progresso and Progresso, CPAs, have asked you, their most knowledgeable systems staff member, to investigate in-house tax preparation from two viewpoints: (1) differential costs and (2) procedural changes. Managing Partner I. M. Progresso thinks the firm could process 60 percent of the returns in-house initially and reach 95 percent by the third year. Some data relevant to your study are:

Number of original returns next year (estimated)	200
Number of returns corrected next year (estimated)	80

*Material from Uniform CPA Examination Questions and Unofficial Answers, Copyright © 1978 by the American Institute of Certified Public Accountants, Inc., is adapted with permission.

Average service bureau cost per return (original and corrected)	$45
Purchase price of tax preparation software	$5,500
Annual software license renewal	$2,600
PC hardware cost per year (capacity of 700 returns)	$5,300
Key input cost per return: original	$4
Key input cost per return: corrected	$1
Supply cost per return printed	$1
Tax practice growth rate per year	20%

Write a memo to I. M. Progresso recommending whether to bring tax preparation in-house. Justify your recommendation on the basis of cost analyses and significant qualitative aspects of changed procedures.[17]

Exercise 8-17
(Tax)

Mark Rood has asked you to prepare his income tax return for the tax year ending December 31, 1991. His records indicate that he received wages and commissions of $30,000 from his job as a salesperson. The records also indicate that Rood did the following during the year:

1. Transferred one-half of his 100 shares of IMP stock, bought in 1989 for $12 a share and worth (on the date of the transfer) $26 a share, to his divorced wife as part of their property settlement.
2. Sold 50 shares of the IMP stock in March of 1991 for $29 a share.
3. Bought a rare Mongolian coin to add to his collection in March of 1991 for $1,000. In August, he sold the coin for $1,800.
4. Bought a Ghanian coin for $2,500 in September and sold it in November for $1,000.

Assuming these are Rood's only capital assets transactions during the year, what is his adjusted gross income?

Write a memo to Rood's file in which you answer this question. Be sure to show the step-by-step computation of his gains and losses.[18]

Exercise 8-18
(Tax)

The George Valentine Company's current earnings and profits were $2,000,000 during the year. Has the company made a distribution of taxable dividends in any of the following transactions? Explain.

1. The company owns and rents a luxury apartment building. It rents one of its 5-room apartments to its major stockholder at 30 percent less than its fair rental value.
2. The company loans $80,000 to its 50 percent shareholder to help him buy a home. In return, the shareholder gives the company a personal note as security for the loan and is charged a reasonable rate of interest (equivalent to the applicable federal rate). The company carries the loan on its books as an account receivable.
3. Mr. George Valentine was the founder and the former chairman of the board of the company. He retired 10 years ago, having been adequately compensated during

the years of his active service. He still owns 100 percent of the company stock. He was paid a fee of $100,000 this year even though he had not been active in business since his retirement.

Write a memo to the client file of the George Valentine Company. Analyze each transaction, and explain why it is or is not a distribution of taxable dividends.[19]

NOTES

1. Thomas M. Barton, "Writing Assignment for Intermediate Accounting" (unpublished class assignment, University of Georgia, 1987).
2. Pete Wardlaw, "Purchasing DCL Broadcasting" (unpublished student paper, University of Georgia, 1987).
3. Ray M. Sommerfeld, G. Fred Streuling, Robert L. Gardner, and Dave N. Stewart, *Tax Research Techniques,* 3rd ed., Revised (New York: American Institute of Certified Public Accountants, 1989), pp. 160–62.
4. Adapted from Sommerfeld, et al., p. 161.
5. Reprinted by permission, from pp. 490–491 in *Modern Auditing* by Walter G. Kell and Richard E. Ziegler. Copyright © 1980 by John Wiley & Sons, Inc.
6. Gordon S. May, "Writing Assignment for Intermediate Accounting" (unpublished class assignment, University of Georgia, 1987).
7. William R. Pasewark, "Writing Assignment for Intermediate Accounting" (unpublished class assignment, University of Georgia, 1987).
8. Adapted from Charles T. Horngren and Walter T. Harrison, *Accounting* (Englewood Cliffs, N.J.: Prentice Hall, Inc., 1989), pp. 36–37. Reprinted by permission.
9. William R. Pasewark, "Writing Assignment for Intermediate Accounting" (unpublished class assignment, University of Georgia, 1987).
10. Gordon S. May, "Writing Assignment for Intermediate Accounting" (unpublished class assignment, University of Georgia, 1990).
11. Adapted from American Institute of Certified Public Accountants, *Uniform CPA Exam: Questions and Unofficial Answers,* November 1988 (New York: American Institute of Certified Public Accountants, 1989), p. 55.
12. Gadis J. Dillon, "Writing Assignment for Intermediate Accounting" (unpublished class assignment, University of Georgia, 1982).
13. Gordon S. May, "Writing Assignment for Intermediate Accounting" (unpublished class assignment, University of Georgia, 1982).
14. Charles T. Horngren, *Introduction to Financial Accounting* (Englewood Cliffs, N.J.: Prentice-Hall, Inc., ©1981), p. 336. Reprinted by permission.
15. Adapted from American Institute of Certified Public Accountants, *Uniform CPA Exam: Questions and Unofficial Answers,* November 1988 (New York: American Institute of Certified Public Accountants, 1989), p. 34.
16. Charles T. Horngren, *Introduction to Management Accounting,* 5th edition (Englewood Cliffs, N.J.: Prentice-Hall, Inc., © 1981), p. 110. Reprinted by permission.
17. Fay Borthick, "Writing Assignment" (unpublished class assignment, University of Tennessee, 1987).
18. Adapted from Prentice-Hall, *1988 Federal Tax Course* (Englewood Cliffs, N.J.: Prentice-Hall, Inc., © 1987), p. 162. Reprinted by permission.
19. Ibid., p. 279.

9

REPORTS

In some situations accountants may need to prepare formal reports. A CPA may prepare a report for a client. Managerial accountants may prepare a report for another department within their firm or perhaps for a group of managers with a particular need. A report usually involves analysis of an accounting problem and application of accounting principles to a particular situation. It may also require some research of the professional literature or other material, so the research techniques discussed in Chapter 10 are often part of a report's preparation.

Reports will vary in length, but all reports should meet certain basic criteria. The accounting content should be accurate, the organization should be coherent, the report should be presented attractively, and the writing style should be clear and concise.

PLANNING A REPORT

The analysis of a report's purpose and audience may be more difficult than it is for letters and memos. A report may have many groups of readers, and each group will have different interests and needs.

For example, a report recommending that a firm invest in a new computer system might be circulated to the MIS department, the accounting department, the various departments that would actually use the system, and senior management. The accounting department would, of course, be interested in the accounting aspects of the acquisition as well as how the system could be used for various accounting tasks. The MIS department would be interested in the technical features of the system and how it would affect MIS personnel. Other departments would want to know how the system would make their work easier or more difficult, whether it would affect their budgets, and whether their personnel would have the training to use the system. Senior management, on the other hand, would be interested in a bigger picture, such as how the system would affect the firm's efficiency, competitiveness, and cash flow.

If you were writing this report, you would need to identify clearly who the readers would be and what information they would want the report to include. You would obviously be writing to readers with different degrees of knowledge about the technical aspects of the new system and with different interests and concerns as well. The way to handle this complicated situation is to write different parts of the report for different groups of readers.

Fortunately, many reports are not as difficult to plan and write as this one would be. But this example shows how important it is to analyze carefully the purposes and readers of the report when you are planning its contents.

Most reports require a great deal of research. They may report the results of empirical studies or pilot projects, or report research involving technical literature or generally accepted accounting principles. Organizing this research into a coherent outline is essential. Review the principles of organization discussed in Chapter 3, and then apply the following questions to your report as you are planning the outline and structuring your draft.

1. Is the subject covered adequately?
   - background information when necessary
   - adequate explanations, supporting data, and examples
   - citations from GAAP and other authorities, as needed
   - application to the specific needs and interests of the readers
2. Is the report too long?
   - digressions—off the subject
   - too much explanation or detail
   - repetitions or wordiness
3. Is the report organized logically?
   - in order from most to least important—from the readers' point of view
   - summary sentences where helpful
   - transitions to link ideas
   - short, well-organized paragraphs with topic sentences

The format of a report, how its various parts are put together, will also make it more coherent.

THE PARTS OF A REPORT

There are a variety of report formats, but they are all designed to make the report easy to read. The format presented in this handbook is typical of the ways in which reports are structured.

A report may include the following parts:

transmittal document
title page
table of contents
list of illustrations
summary section
introduction
body of the report
conclusion
appendices
notes
bibliography

Transmittal Document

The transmittal document can be either a letter or memo, depending on whether you are sending your report to someone outside your organization or within it. This document is a cover letter or memo: it presents the report to the people for whom it was written and adds any other information that will be helpful.

The transmittal document will not be long, but it should include some essential information: the report's title, what it is about, and why it was written. It is usually a good idea to summarize the main idea or recommendation of the report, if you can do so in about one or two sentences. You may want to add other comments about the report that will be helpful to the readers, but always end with a courteous closing.

While the style of the actual report is usually formal and impersonal, the transmittal document can usually be more conversational, including the use of personal pronouns.

Title Page

In a report prepared in a professional situation, the title page may look something like this:

Title of Report
Prepared for. . .
Prepared by. . .
Date

For a student report, the instructor may prefer information such as this:

Title of Report
Student's Name
Course and Period
Instructor
Date

Table of Contents

The table of contents should be on a separate page and should have a heading. The contents listed will be the major parts of the report, excluding the transmittal document, with the appropriate page numbers.

List of Illustrations

The list of illustrations, if applicable, will include titles and page numbers of graphs, charts, and other illustrations.

Summary Section

All formal reports should have a section at the beginning of the report that summarizes the main ideas and recommendations. This section can vary in length from one paragraph to several pages, and it can come either immediately before or immediately after the introduction. The summary section may be called an executive summary, abstract, synopsis, summary, or some other term.

An executive summary is especially helpful for long reports. This section gives the readers an overview of the report's contents without the technical detail. Busy managers may read the executive summary to decide whether they should read the entire report.

The executive summary will identify the purpose and scope of the report and possibly the methods used for research. It will include the major findings of the research, the conclusions of the researcher, and the recommendations, if any.

The length of an executive summary will vary with the length of the report, but it is generally about one to three double-spaced pages. It should begin on a separate page following the table of contents or list of illustrations, and should be entitled *Executive Summary*. The sample report at the end of this chapter uses this kind of summary.

For shorter reports, a section right after the introduction can provide a summary of the report's main ideas and recommendations. This section should be labeled *Summary;* it will usually be one or two paragraphs long.

Introduction

The introduction of a formal report is longer than that for a letter or memo. It will probably be at least two or three short paragraphs, and for long reports may even be longer than a page.

The introduction should identify the subject of the report and may state why it was written—who requested or authorized it, or for whom it was prepared. The introduction should state the purpose of the report in specific terms:

> The purpose of this report is to discuss the feasibility of offering a stock bonus plan to employees of Greenpine Industries.
> NOT: The purpose of this report is to discuss stock bonus plans.

Sometimes the introduction will include additional information to help the reader. It may, for example, give a brief background of the report's topic. However, if it's necessary to include very much background information, this material should be presented in a separate section within the body of the report.

Finally, the introduction of a report should end with a plan of development that gives the reader an overview of the topics the report will cover in the order they will be presented. A simple plan of development may be in sentence form:

> This report will describe the proposed pension plan and then discuss its costs and benefits.

However, sometimes a set-off list makes the plan of development easier to read:

> This report will discuss the following topics related to the proposed pension plan:
> * Major provisions
> * Benefits to employees
> * Benefits to the corporation
> * Cost
> * Accounting for the plan

Body of the Report

The body of the report should be divided into sections and possibly subsections, each with an appropriate heading. Remember to begin each section with a statement that summarizes the main idea to be covered in that section.

Conclusion

In addition to the summary section at the beginning, a report should have a conclusion to remind the reader of the report's main ideas and conclusions. Depending on the length of the report, the conclusion may be from one paragraph to several pages.

Appendices (optional)

Depending on the report's audience and purpose, you may want to place highly technical information, statistics, etc., in appendices at the end of the report. If you use an appendix, give it a title and refer to it in the body of the report.

End Matter

What to put at the end of the report depends in part on the style of documentation you use. If you use endnotes, they should begin on a separate page and be labeled *Notes.*

Almost all reports will have some sort of bibliography or reference list. This list will identify the sources you cited within your paper, and it may also include additional references that the reader might wish to consult. This section should begin on a separate page following the notes (if any), and should have a title such as *Bibliography* or *References.*

Chapter 10 demonstrates the proper form for endnotes and bibliographical entries.

Graphic Illustrations

If your report contains much statistical or numerical data, graphic illustrations will make it more interesting and easiser to read. Graphs, such as the one on page 98, are useful to make comparisons or to show trends. Tables or charts summarize numerical data efficiently.

Graphic illustrations should be numbered and have a descriptive title. They should be labeled so that the reader can understand them without reading the main text of the report. On the other hand, they should be discussed and interpreted within the body of the report, with references to the number of the illustration:

A comparison of the previous five years' earnings for the three departments shows Department B to be the top performer (see Figure 6-1).

You can place graphic illustrations either in an appendix or in the body of your report, just after the place in the text where they are discussed.

APPEARANCE

It is important to present your report as attractively as possible. Use good quality paper and be sure that the report is neatly typed or printed. Corrections should be few and unobtrusive.

Reports should be double spaced, with the exception of the transmittal document and any set-off material. Pages should be numbered, using lower case Roman numerals for prefatory pages (table of contents, list of illustrations, executive summary) and Arabic numerals for the remainder of the report, from the introduction through the end matter.

STYLE AND TONE

The tone of a formal report should usually be just what its names implies—formal, and therefore impersonal. You probably would not, for example, use personal pronouns, or contractions.

However, a formal style should still be readable and interesting, so you should use the techniques of effective style discussed in Chapter 4. Even a formal document can be written simply, clearly, and concretely.

In contrast with the actual report, the transmittal document may be written in a personal, more informal style.

The report in Figure 9–1 illustrates many of these techniques of effective report writing.[1]

EXERCISES

Write reports for the following situations. Invent any details you need to make the reports complete.

Exercise 9–1
(all levels)

One of your clients, Albert P. Moneybags, III, has recently inherited a portfolio of stocks in various Fortune 500 companies. He has received the annual reports of these companies, which of course include the income statement, balance sheet, statement of cash flows, and statement of retained earnings.

Albert knows very little about these statements. He has asked you to write a report that will explain the statements so that he can use them to manage his investments.

Prepare the report for your client. Supplement your discussion with sample financial statements that you construct yourself or find in the annual report of an actual company.

Execise 9–2
(all levels)

The board of directors of Top Flite Golf Equipment Company is meeting to evaluate the company's performance for the year just ended. Suppose the report in Figure 9–2, which applies to Top Flite's basic line of golf clubs, has been prepared for use at the meeting.

The directors are disappointed at the net income results. They ask if the company maintained the price of its golf clubs at the budgeted sale price of $120, and they are told yes. Moreover, the levels of beginning and ending inventories were unchanged. (Continued on page 167.)

```
                                                    Bryan and Howard, CPAs
                                                    125 Easy Street
                                                    Athens, Georgia
                                                    August 8, 1992


Mr. Sam Hamilton
Hamilton Manufacturing
1890 Meerly Avenue
Atlanta, Georgia  30306

Dear Mr. Hamilton:

        Enclosed is the report about convertible bonds which you requested in
your letter of July 21.  The report, entitled Convertible Bonds: Financial
and Accounting Considerations, examines the nature of convertible debt, the
pros and cons of such an issue, and the accounting treatment of the securities.

        As you suggested, I have discussed the accounting standards (GAAP) affect-
ing convertible debt.  Two Opinions of the Accounting Principles Board, Nos.
14 and 15, have particular bearing on convertible debt; each is logical, but
the logic of one is quite inconsistent with the logic of the other.  I believe
that you will find the standards interesting.

        I believe the report will provide you with the information you need.
If you have any further questions, however, don't hesitate to give me a call.




                                                    Sincerely yours,

                                                    Jean Bryan

                                                    Jean Bryan






jhw
```

FIGURE 9-1 A Report

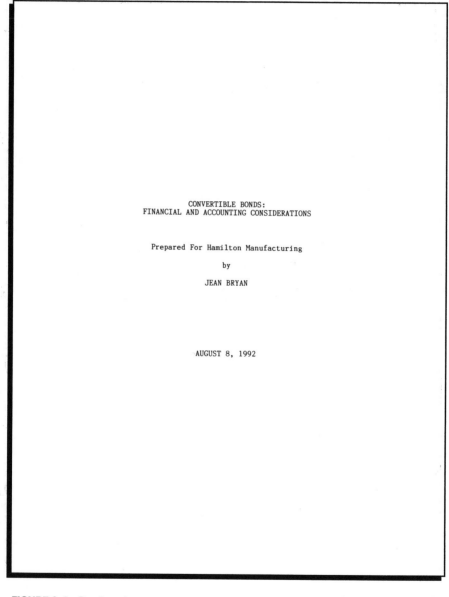

CONVERTIBLE BONDS:
FINANCIAL AND ACCOUNTING CONSIDERATIONS

Prepared For Hamilton Manufacturing

by

JEAN BRYAN

AUGUST 8, 1992

FIGURE 9-1 Continued

CONTENTS

i

FIGURE 9-1 Continued

EXECUTIVE SUMMARY

This report provides information about convertible bonds for the managers of Hamilton Manufacturing. Included is information about the nature of convertible bonds, financial advantages and disadvantages Hamilton could expect from issuing such bonds, and their accounting treatment.

A convertible bond is a debt security that carries the option of exchange for an equity security, usually common stock. The bond indenture specifies when the bonds may be converted and a conversion price or ratio. The conversion price is usually from 10 to 20 percent above the market price of the common stock at the time of issue. Both the issuer and the investor expect the market price of the stock to rise above the conversion price; therefore, bondholders are likely to convert the bond into equity.

Convertible bonds would offer Hamilton three advantages:

° The company could issue the bonds at a premium or at a low stated interest rate, which investors would accept because of the conversion privilege.

° The company could avoid another stock issue now, when the price of Hamilton's stock is low.

° Management would avoid possible conflict with its major stockholder.

There are also potential disadvantages which management should consider before issuing the convertible bonds:

° The uncertain conditions of the economy make a future increase in the market price of the company's stock uncertain. If conversion does not occur, Hamilton may have difficulty meeting the debt requirements.

° Bond conversion will reduce earnings per share and operating leverage. Conversion will also increase Hamilton's income tax liability because of the loss of interest expense.

FIGURE 9-1 Continued

    ° The required accounting treatment of convertible bonds, which is deter-
      mined by Accounting Principles Board Opinions 14 and 15, may create
      an unfavorable effect on the company's financial statements: a high
      level of debt may be presented alongside a lowered earnings per share.

iii

FIGURE 9-1   Continued

CONVERTIBLE BONDS: FINANCIAL AND ACCOUNTING CONSIDERATIONS

Introduction

The purpose of this report is to provide information for the management of Hamilton Manufacturing about an increasingly popular form of financing: convertible debt. Convertible debt is an issue of debt securities (bonds) that carry the option of exchange for equity securities (usually common stock).

The primary focus of the report is the accounting requirements for convertible debt and the reasons for the requirements.

Four major topics make up the report: (1) The nature of convertible bonds, (2) financial advantages and disadvantages Hamilton could expect if it issues the bonds, (3) accounting treatment, and (4) logic of the accounting requirements.

Nature of Convertible Bonds

When convertible bonds are issued, the bond indenture specifies a period of time after issuance during which the bonds may be converted. The indenture also specifies a conversion price, "the amount of par value of principal amount of the bonds exchangeable for one share of stock" [Bogen, 1968, p. 31]. If a conversion ratio, rather than a conversion price, is specified, the effective price of stock to the bondholder may be determined by dividing the par value of the bond by the number of shares exchangeable for one bond.

The conversion price, which is determined when the bonds are sold, is usually from 10 to 20 percent above the prevailing market price of the common stock at the time of issue. Both the issuing firm and the investor expect that the market price of the stock will rise above the conversion price, and

1

FIGURE 9–1 Continued

that the conversion privilege will then be exercised by most or all bondholders.

The indenture typically includes a call provision so that the issuing firm can force bondholders to convert. Therefore, it is evident that firms issuing convertible debt often truly want to raise equity capital. The reasons that they choose convertible debt are discussed below.

Financial Advantages and Disadvantages

Advantages

The use of convertible debt would offer Hamilton advantages over straight debt or stock issues.

Bonds that are convertible into stock are in demand. Therefore, bond buyers are willing to accept a low stated interest rate on such bonds, to pay a premium and accept a lower yield, or to accept less restrictive covenants. Hamilton could thus obtain funds at a lower cost than would be possible if it issued bonds without the conversion privilege.

The advantages of a convertible bond issue over a common stock issue relate to timing. While Hamilton might be willing to take on more equity in the future, current economic conditions make this an unfavorable time to sell stock. One authority has explained this advantage as follows:

> To sell stock now would require giving up more shares to raise a given amount of money than management thinks is necessary. However, setting the conversion price 10 to 20 percent above the present market price of the stock will require giving up 10 to 20 percent fewer shares when the bonds are converted than would be required if stock were sold directly. [Brigham, 1978, p. 532].

Another possible advantage to Hamilton of issuing convertible bonds is that the company could avoid creating a possible conflict with the major stockholder, who would likely want to maintain his controlling interest. The stockholder might vote against a large issue of stock. However, the bond issue could be convertible into a number of shares small enough not to injure significantly the stockholder's interest.

FIGURE 9-1 Continued

Disadvantages

Most of the disadvantages of convertible bonds are related to the uncertainty of the conversion and its timing. If Hamilton's stock price does not rise, conversion will not occur, and the company will not obtain the equity financing it desired. Hamilton might then have difficulty meeting the unplanned-for obligations of debt.

Other disadvantages arise, however, if the conversion does occur. When the debt becomes equity, earnings per share is reduced, operating leverage is reduced, and income taxes rise because interest expense is reduced.

Accounting Treatment

The Accounting Principles Board, in its Opinion No. 14, ruled that convertible bonds "which are sold at a price or have a value at issuance not significantly in excess of the face amount" must be treated in the same manner as other bonds [1969, par. 1]. That is, "no portion of the proceeds from the issuance . . . should be accounted for as attributable to the conversion feature" [par. 10]. The expectation that some or all of the bonds will be converted into stock is not recognized in the accounts.

Since convertible bonds are normally sold at a premium, the amount of the cash proceeds from the issue is greater than the face value of the bonds. The difference between the debit to Cash and the credit to Bonds Payable is credited to a Premium on Bonds account. The premium is amortized, using the effective interest method, over the life of the bonds. The effect of the amortization is that the interest expense recorded by Hamilton each period would not equal the amount of the interest payment, but would reflect the effective yield to the bondholders.

When the bonds are converted, Hamilton will remove from the accounts the balances associated with those bonds: Bonds Payable will be debited for the

FIGURE 9-1 Continued

par value of the bonds converted, and the Premium account will be debited for
the portion of the unamortized premium which is attributable to the bonds converted. Two methods can be used to record the common stock issued in exchange
for the bonds. Under one method, the stock is assigned a value equal to the
market value of the stock or the bonds. If this value differs from the book
value of the bonds (the balances associated with the bonds, mentioned above),
then a gain or a loss is recorded. Under the other method, which is more widely
used, the value assigned to the stock equals the book value of the bonds, and
no gain or loss is recognized or recorded [Kieso and Weygandt, 1989, pp. 756-
757].

If Hamilton decides to retire its convertible bonds for cash before their
maturity date, the transaction will be recorded in the same way as the early
retirement of any other debt. The difference between the book value of the
bonds and the cash paid to retire them will be a gain or a loss. If the gain
or loss is material, it will be shown as an extraordinary item on the income
statement.

While convertibles are accounted for solely as debt, Hamilton must also
consider the equity characteristics of such issues in computing earnings per
share (EPS). APB Opinion No. 15 requires that corporations which have issued
securities that are potentially dilutive of EPS must present, in their financial
statements, two EPS figures. If a convertible security meets the requirements
of certain tests, as outlined in SFAS No. 55, it is considered a common stock
equivalent and enters the calculation of primary EPS; otherwise, it enters
only the calculation of fully diluted EPS [Kieso and Weygandt, 1989, pp. 777-
78].

Both EPS figures represent EPS as if the bonds had been converted into
stock. If they had been converted, the removal of the bonds would have caused
a reduction of interest expense, which would have increased earnings; therefore,

FIGURE 9-1 Continued

Hamilton will have to revise the number of shares upward [Kieso and Weygandt, 1986, pp. 717-719]. However, the positive effect of the earnings adjustment may not offset the negative effect of the shares adjustment. The result is that convertibles reduce reported EPS.

Logic of the Accounting Requirements

In requiring that convertible debt be accounted for solely as debt, the APB reasoned that the debt and the conversion feature are inseparable [Opinion 14, 1969, par. 10]. That is, at any given time, a security is either all debt or all equity. Therefore, since at the time of issuance the security is all debt, its issuance should be recorded as debt.

The Board argued further that practical problems exist in the attempt to value the debt and conversion features separately. The conversion feature is difficult to value because of the uncertainty of the timing of conversion, and because of the uncertain future market value of stock. The debt part of the security is difficult to value independently of the conversion option, because the conversion option affects the terms of the bond. An attempt to value the bonds as if they were not convertible would require the assumption of higher terms--an unrealistic assumption, because the issuing firm would not have wanted to issue bonds with those terms [Opinion 14, 1969, par. 6].

The accounting requirements concerning presentation of EPS are intended to meet investors' reporting needs. In its Opinion No. 15, the APB explains that the value of a convertible security "is derived in large part from the value of the common stock to which it is related," and that the holder of such a security is essentially a participator in "the earnings and earnings potential of the issuing corporation" [1969, par. 25]. Therefore, the determination of EPS based only on outstanding shares of common stock "would place form over substance" [par. 26], and would mislead the investors.

FIGURE 9-1 Continued

Conclusion

In the decision whether to finance with convertible debt, Hamilton must consider whether it would benefit from using convertibles rather than straight debt or stock issues, and whether it can meet the debt requirements, should conversion not occur as expected. In additon, management should analyze carefully the effect of the issue on readers of the financial statements, because until the bonds are converted, a possibly high level of debt will exist alongside a lowered presentation of earnings per share.

FIGURE 9-1   Continued

WORKS CITED

Accounting Principles Board, <u>Accounting for Convertible Debt and Debt Issued with Stock Purchase Warrants</u>, Opinion No. 14 (N.Y. : AICPA, 1969).

Accounting Principles Board, <u>Earnings per Share</u>, Opinion No. 15 (N.Y. : AICPA, 1969).

Bogen, J.I., ed., <u>Financial Handbook</u>, 4th ed. (N.Y. : Ronald Press, 1968).

Booker, J.A., and Jarnagin, B.D., <u>Financial Accounting Standards</u>: <u>Explanation and Analysis</u> (Chicago: Commerce Clearing House, 1979).

Brigham, E.F., <u>Fundamentals of Financial Management</u>, (Hinsdale, Ill.: Dryden Press, 1978).

Financial Accounting Standards Board, <u>Determining Whether a Convertible Security Is a Common Stock Equivalent</u>, Statement of Financial Accounting Standards No. 55 (Stamford, Conn. : FASB, 1982).

Kieso, D.E., and Weygandt, J.J., <u>Intermediate Accounting</u>, 6th ed., (N.Y. : Wiley, 1989).

FIGURE 9-1 Continued

Top Flite Golf Equipment Co.
Performance Report
Year End June 30, 19X7

	ACTUAL RESULTS	MASTER BUDGET	VARIANCE	
Sales	$2,655,000	$3,240,000	$585,000	U
Variable expenses:				
Cost of goods sold	$1,189,000	$1,546,000	$357,000	F
Promotion expense	126,800	110,000	16,800	U
Sales commissions	116,900	166,000	49,100	F
Shipping	64,000	87,000	23,000	F
Utilities	13,000	14,000	1,000	F
Fixed expenses:				
Salaries	341,600	439,000	97,400	F
Depreciation	306,000	313,000	7,000	F
Rent	143,500	171,000	27,500	F
Utilities	11,200	13,000	1,800	F
Total operating expenses	2,312,000	2,859,000	547,000	F
Income before income tax	343,000	381,000	38,000	U
Income tax expense (30%)	102,900	114,300	11,400	F
Net income	$ 240,100	$ 266,700	$ 26,600	U

FIGURE 9-2   Performance Report for Exercise 9-2

Required

1. Use the above information to prepare a more informative performance report. Hint: Begin by computing actual sales volume in units. Then prepare a flexible budget based on this actual volume.
2. A downturn in the economy was responsible for the company's inability to sell more golf clubs. How would you view company performance in light of this additional information? Would you decide to overhaul operations or keep the business operating on its present course? Consider how people adjust their spending on luxury items like golf clubs during a recession.[2]

Write a report for Top Flight's Board of Directors. Your report should include the performance report you have prepared as well as your discussion of the topics in the second requirement above.

Exercise 9-3
(Intermediate)

You have received an inquiry from a prospective client, Johnson Marketing, Inc., concerning the accounting for inventories. Johnson is in the process of establishing a very large mail order business that will require a large inventory of miscellaneous items to be sold at different markups. Write a report for Bill Johnson, the president of this company, explaining briefly the various options of accounting for inventories and their effects. Remember that your client is *not* an accountant and knows very little about accounting.[3]

Exercise 9-4
(Intermediate)

Smith and Jones are planning to open a new downtown shoe store. Mr. Smith has heard of the FIFO, LIFO, specific identification, and lower-of-cost-or-market methods of valuing inventory, but does not understand them. Since you will be the accountant for the partnership, Smith has asked you to prepare a report recommending an appropriate method for valuing the inventory. Jones has asked that the report describe the advantages and disadvantages of each method, from both practical and theoretical perspectives.[4]

Exercise 9-5
(Intermediate or Auditing)

Write a report in response to the letter in Figure 9-3.[5]

Exercise 9-6
(Intermediate or Auditing)

Write a report in response to the letter in Figure 9-4.[6]

Exercise 9-7
(Accounting Information Systems)

Select a small business in your community that plans to improve its accounting system. Analyze the business's needs for an accounting system, including the possibility of a microcomputer.

This project will probably require you to interview the business's management so that you understand how the business operates, what its systems needs are, and the budgetary constraints within which management will be working.

You may decide, after evaluating the business's needs, that it does not need a microcomputer at the present time. If this is the case, write a five- or ten-year systems plan based on projected growth of the business.

If you do conclude that the business should purchase a microcomputer, what hardware and software do you recommend?

If the business already has a computer system, should it scrap the present system or update it?

Write your evaluation and recommendation in the form of a report to the business's manager or owner.

```
                                         Office of the Controller
                                         Southern Cement
                                         1021 Peachtree Ave.
                                         Atlanta, GA  30309

                                         January 10, 1992


Mary L. De Quincy
Auditor-in-Charge
Lewis and Clark, C.P.A.s
111 Baxter St.
Athens, GA  30605

Dear Ms. De Quincy:

     Last year's fiscal year will be the fifteenth year that you have audited
our financial statements.  I appreciate the work you have done for us.

     As you know, the company has been growing steadily since our inception
75 years ago.  The last 10 years have been particularly good because of
Atlanta's tremendous growth in condominiums.  Continued growth has required
us to purchase at a rapid rate machinery to mix and pour cement at construction
sites.  Almost all of our machinery has been financed by Confederate National
Bank.  Until now, the bank has been eager to lend us money at the prime rate
when using the machines as collateral.

     Southern Cement usually makes large down payments from contract proceeds
on equipment purchases.  Lately we have experienced equipment purchasing prob-
lems because our contracts do not require payment until the contract is com-
plete.  We have recently accepted some long-term contracts that will be quite
lucrative, but we will not receive payment for two years.  There is no reason
to believe that we will not be paid eventually.

     Confederate National refused to make additional equipment loans to us
because it believes we are "over-leveraged."  The loan officer supports this
refusal by calling attention to our debt-to-equity ratio, which is higher than
those of our competitors.

     Southern Cement's liabilities are higher than the liabilities of our com-
petitors due to one account -- deferred taxes.  The deferred taxes account
is higher for Southern Cement for two reasons:

     (1)  Our company is older than the competitors and deferred taxes have
          accumulated over a number of years.

     (2)  Tax advantages from accelerated depreciation on equipment purchases
          in the last 10 years have allowed us to defer large amounts of tax
          payments.
```

FIGURE 9-3 Letter for Exercise 9-5.

Mary L. De Quincy
January 10, 1992
Page 2

I do not expect this account to decline in the future since our company continues to require additional equipment. Quite frankly, I have never seen the need to include deferred taxes in the liability section of the balance sheet since it is highly unlikely that these amounts will ever be paid to the federal government. Deferred taxes that become due have always been replaced by a greater amount that will be deferred. The deferred tax account has continued to grow at a steady rate. Removal of deferred taxes that will not become due would significantly reduce Southern Cement's debt-to-equity ratio enough to convince any banker to make an additional equipment loan to us.

In the last three years, several other CPA firms have approached me to solicit our account. Out of curiousity I recently asked one of them whether it would be possible to issue an unqualified opinion on a balance sheet prepared without deferred taxes as a liability. A member of one firm claimed that he saw no problems; however, his firm would require an additional fee to cover research costs in financial statement preparation. Since I am reluctant to change accountants, is it possible for you to prepare the financial statements without including deferred taxes? The absence of deferred taxes would provide the following advantages.

(1) Eliminate a "false liability" which misleads our creditors and stockholders.

(2) Reduce our debt-to-equity ratio, thereby allowing us to obtain our desperately needed loan.

I have never fully understood the disclosure requirements for deferred taxes. I do believe, however, that the elimination of this account from our balance sheet would result in a more accurate representation of our financial position. I would appreciate a detailed analysis of your position on this proposal.

Sincerely,

Sandy Loam
Sandy Loam
Controller

FIGURE 9-3 Continued

Office of the Controller
Internal Furnishings, Inc.
Dallas, Texas 77840

September 30, 1992

B.B. May
Auditor-in-Charge
External Accounting Partners
Dallas, Texas 77841

Dear B.B.:

It has been almost a year since you helped us set up a noncontributory defined
benefit pension program for our employees. You are aware that our company
has been moderately profitable in the past few years and we do not expect this
trend to change in the next five years (a trend that should provide adequate
funds for the pension plan). While we are all excited about the prospects
of retiring rich, there have been some problems with the implementation of
the pension system and the recording of pension transactions. As consultant
to our pension plan project, you may be able to help us by addressing the
following:

(1) I am unclear about the role of the actuary in the pension plan process.
Could you please describe what an actuary is and what tasks we should expect
an actuary to perform in our pension plan? You also mentioned that actuarial
gains and losses can occur in pension accounting. Please describe how these
gains and losses occur and the different methods we can use to account for
these costs.

(2) You probably remember that we allocated $500,000 for five years of past
service cost. You explained to me that normal cost liabilities relate to qualified employee service <u>after</u> the inception of the plan and past service costs
relate to qualified employee services <u>before</u> the inception of the plan. I
suggest that in order to abide by the matching concept we expense normal pension
costs after the pension inception date and expense past service costs before
the inception date. Past service costs could be deducted (debited) from retained earnings. If this is a violation of generally accepted accounting
principles, pleast let me know the correct procedure and why it is better than
my way.

FIGURE 9-4 Letter for Exercise 9-6.

B.B. May
September 30, 1992
Page 2

(3) I read that a pension expense must be between maximum and minimum limits. These limits do not seem difficult to calculate; however, I am curious about why they exist. Would you please explain to me in simple terms the purpose of maximum and minimum limits and how they were developed?

Thank you for your help.

Sincerely,

Art Deco

Art Deco
Controller

FIGURE 9-4   Continued

NOTES

1. Adapted from Jean Bryan, "Financial and Accounting Considerations of Issuing Convertible Debt" (unpublished student paper, University of Georgia, 1980).
2. Adapted from Charles T. Horngren and Walter T. Harrison, *Accounting* (Englewood Cliffs, N.J.: Prentice Hall, Inc., 1989), pp. 969-70. Reprinted by permission.
3. Gordon S. May, "Writing Assignment for Intermediate Accounting" (unpublished class assignment, University of Georgia, 1982).
4. Randolph A. Shockley, "Writing Assignment for Intermediate Accounting," (unpublished class assignment, University of Georgia, 1982).
5. William R. Pasewark, "Writing Assignment for Intermediate Accounting" (unpublished class assignment, University of Georgia, 1986).
6. Ibid.

10

RESEARCH PAPERS

Sometimes accountants need to research accounting pronouncements or other literature as one step in the preparation of a report or other document. This research may involve an in-depth look at official pronouncements, such as the Opinions of the Accounting Principles Board (APB) or Statements of the Financial Accounting Standards Board (FASB). Sometimes, too, accountants must research the details of government regulations, such as provisions of the Internal Revenue Code. They also read other kinds of professional literature, such as journal articles, public documents, and monographs on topics of current interest.

This chapter discusses, in an elementary step-by-step approach, how to write a research paper. Much of the material will be review for students or professionals who have written term papers or documented reports. However, the suggestions should be helpful to anyone who must research the professional literature and then summarize the results of that research in a written form.

HOW TO START

If you are writing a paper that requires research of the literature, chances are you already know something about the topic. If you don't, or if your memory is only vague, do some initial reading so that you have a basic familiarity with your subject. An accounting textbook may be a good place to start.

Once you have a general idea of what your topic involves, you will need to look for additional information. Often the next step will be to look at official accounting pronouncements, such as those found in *Accounting Standards: Current Text.*[1] Or you may need to study government regulations or laws to find out how to handle a client's technical problem. For either case, read the material carefully and take accurate notes of your findings, including references to the sources you are using. A later section of this chapter discusses note taking in more detail.

Some research papers will require a search for additional source materials in the library. It's a good idea to consult a librarian to see what help is available to you. Most libraries now have computer search facilities and staff who will work with you to help you find the materials you need.

One reference that you may find in the library is the *Accountant's Index,*[2] which lists articles published in accounting periodicals. The index is arranged chronologically in volumes covering perhaps half a year. Within each volume, the articles are grouped according to topic and author. Be imaginative in looking for articles on your topic; consider the different headings it could be listed under. For example, "Stock rights" might be listed as "Fractional share rights," "Share rights," or "Stock warrants."

The library will likely have other references as well that you may find helpful. For example, many newspapers, including *The Wall Street Journal,* publish an index. Many of these indices are available as both reference books and computerized reference services.

The librarian can help you find these and other references that will help you prepare your paper.

NOTE TAKING

Once you have located a useful source, take notes on what you read. For this step in your research you will need two sets of cards—3 × 5 ″ cards for the bibliography and 4 × 6 ″ (or 5 × 8 ″) cards for the notes. Using these cards will save time and trouble in the long run, even though they may seem like a bother at the time you are reading. They will help you keep track of your sources and notes, and they will be easy to use when you write your draft.

Let's look first at a bibliography card, which is illustrated in Figure 10-1.

Be sure that you include on the card all the information you will need for your bibliography (see "Documentation," later in this chapter). It is frustrating to make an extra trip to the library just to check on a date or page number.

Note cards contain the information you will actually use in your paper. Notice the parts of the note card in Figure 10-2.[3] The numbers in the upper right-hand corner give the source (from the bibliography card) and the page(s) where this information was found. The heading gives you an idea of what this note card is about. The note itself is taken from the source. It is the material you will use in your paper. The outline code corresponds with the section in your outline where the note fits in.

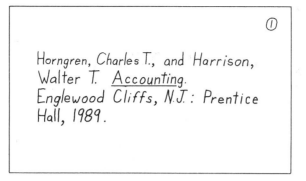

FIGURE 10-1 Bibliography Card

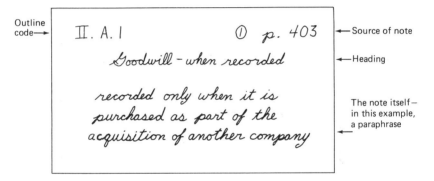

FIGURE 10-2 Note Card

DIRECT QUOTATION AND PARAPHRASE

You can take notes in two ways, as a direct quotation (the exact words from the source) or as a paraphrase (your words and sentence structures). It's usually much better to take the notes in your own words. If you take the time to paraphrase as you research, you will save time when you write your draft.

Here is a good way to paraphrase. Read a section from your source—perhaps several short paragraphs. Then look away from the page and try to remember the important ideas. Write them down. Then look back at your source to check your notes for accuracy.

Occasionally you may want to use a direct quotation. When you copy a quotation on a note card, use quotation marks so you'll know later that these are someone else's words. Copy the quotation *exactly,* including capitalization and punctuation.

It's important that direct quotations be accurate and that paraphrases be your own words and sentence structures, not just a slight variation of your source.

It's also important to give credit for material you borrow from another writer. If you don't, you'll be guilty of plagiarism. *The Harbrace College Handbook* contains the following discussion of plagiarism:

> If you fail to acknowledge borrowed material, then you are plagiarizing. Plagiarism is literary theft. When you copy the words of another, be sure to put those words inside quotation marks and to acknowledge the source with a footnote. When you paraphrase the words of another, use your own words and your own sentence structure, and be sure to give a footnote citing the source of the idea. A plagiarist often merely changes a few words or rearranges the words of the source. As you take notes and as you write your paper, be especially careful to avoid plagiarism.[4]

The *MLA Handbook* defines plagiarism as "the act of using another person's writing without acknowledging the source."[5] The most obvious form of plagiarism is to use another person's words, but sometimes plagiarism is more subtle:

> Other forms of plagiarism include repeating someone else's particularly apt phrase without appropriate acknowledgment, paraphrasing another person's argument as your own, and presenting another's line of thinking in the development of an idea as though it were your own.[6]

The key to avoiding plagiarism, of course, is to document your sources adequately with either internal documentation or notes (see the Documentation section which follows). In actual practice, however, there may be situations when you will not know whether you should identify the source of information you wish to use in your paper. The difficulty arises because information that is considered "common knowledge" in a given field need not be documented.

Obviously the problem is to decide what is "common knowledge." One rule of thumb says that if you can find the same information in three different sources, that information is considered common knowledge and therefore need not be documented.

There are indeed many grey areas when it comes to issues of plagiarism. Perhaps the safest rule is to document your sources whenever there is any question of possible plagiarism.

THE OUTLINE

As you are taking notes, you will probably form some idea of the major divisions of the paper. That is, you should be getting a rough idea of its outline.

Go ahead and write down your ideas for an outline. The more reading you do, the more complete the outline will become. Stop and evaluate the outline from time to time. Are you covering all the important areas of your topic? Is the outline getting too long? Should you narrow the topic? Are some sections of the outline irrelevant to the topic? Answering these questions will guide you as you continue your research.

Once your research is complete, or nearly so, you should refine your outline. Be sure that your topic is covered completely and that the ideas are arranged in the most effective order. Think about the introduction and conclusion to your paper, and any other relevant parts. For example, do you want to include charts, tables, or graphs?

Next, arrange the note cards in the order of the outline, and write the outline code in the upper left-hand corner of the card.

With a completed outline and an orderly stack of note cards, you are ready to write the draft.

THE DRAFT

The draft of a research paper is written just like that of any other kind of writing, with the exception that you are incorporating note cards into your own ideas. If you have already paraphrased the notes, your task is much easier.

You do need to include in your draft an indication of where your notes came from. In other words, you want to give credit for words or ideas that are not your own. In the final version of your paper, these references will be footnotes, endnotes, or parenthetical citations. In the draft, you can indicate your sources with a parenthetical notation like this: (① p. 403). The numbers come from the note card and refer to the source and page number of the note.

REVISING

After you have completed the draft of your research paper, you will need to revise it to perfect the organization, development, style, grammar, and spelling. It may also be a good idea to have a colleague review your paper and suggest ways it can be improved.

DOCUMENTATION

Any information you get from a source other than your own knowledge must be documented; that is, you must say where you got the information. Styles for documentation vary, but we will look at two of the most common, internal documentation and notes.[7]

Internal Documentation

Many writers prefer to use internal documentation, which places information about sources within the text, using brackets [ ] or parentheses ( ). What goes within the brackets depends on the kind of source you are using. The list which follows gives sample citations for sources typically used by accountants. For further information on internal documentation, you can consult *The Chicago Manual of Style*[8] or the *Publication Manual of the American Psychological Association.*[9]

It's a good idea to introduce quotations or paraphrases within the text itself:

> *According to ARB 43,* current assets are "reasonably expected to be realized in cash or sold or consumed during the normal operating cycle of the business" [Ch. 3A, par. 4].

Information you include in the introduction to the quotation or paraphrase does not need to be repeated within the brackets. Thus in this example, *ARB 43* was left out of the brackets, since it was mentioned in the introductory phrase.

Notice also that the end punctuation for the quotation, in this case the period, comes after the brackets.

One reminder about the use of technical sources such as this one Consider whether the readers of your paper will be familiar with the literature cited. If they aren't, it's helpful to identify the source more fully and possibly give a brief explanation of its significance.

At the end of your paper you will need a reference list that identifies fully, in alphabetical order, the sources you cited within your paper. Sample entries for this list appear below, along with typical citations that you would use within the text.

INTERNAL DOCUMENTATION

C = Citation within the text
R = Entry in reference list

Book

C   [Horngren and Harrison, 1992, p. 403]
R   Horngren, C. T., and Harrison, W. T., *Accounting,* 2nd ed. (Englewood Cliffs, N.J.: Prentice Hall, 1992).

Article in a Journal

C   [Bamber, 1987]
R   Bamber, L. S., "Unexpected Earnings, Firm Size, and Trading Volume Around Quarterly Earnings Announcements," *The Accounting Review* (July 1987), pp. 510–532.

APB Opinion

C   [Opinion 25, 1972, par. 10]
R   Accounting Principles Board, *Accounting for Stock Issued to Employees,* Opinion No. 25 (N.Y.: AICPA, 1972).

FASB—Financial Accounting Standard

C   [SFAS 5, 1975, par. 15]
R   Financial Accounting Standards Board, *Accounting for Contingencies,* Statement of Financial Accounting Standards No. 5. (Stamford, CT: FASB, 1975).

FASB—Financial Accounting Concept

C   [SFAC 1, 1978, par. 3]
R   Financial Accounting Standards Board, *Objectives of Financial Reporting by Business Enterprises,* Statement of Financial Accounting Concepts No. 1 (Stamford, CT: FASB, 1978).

Primary Source Reprinted in Current Text

C   [SFAC 1, 1978, par. 3]
R   Financial Accounting Standards Board, *Objectives of Financial Reporting by Business Enterprises,* Statement of Financial Accounting Concepts No. 1 (Stamford, CT: FASB, 1978), as reported in *Accounting Standards: Current Text as of June 1, 1990* (Homewood, Ill.: Irwin, 1990).

Legal Citation

C   [Aaron v. SEC, 446 U.S. 680(1980)]
R   Same form as citation.

IRS—Code Section

C   [Sec. 6111(a)]
R   Internal Revenue Code. Sec. 6111(a).

Federal Register

C   [48 Fed. Reg., 1983, p. 52, 579]
C   "Establishment of Sonoma County Green Valley Vitacultural Area, Final Rule." *Federal Register* 48 (Nov. 21, 1983).

Endnotes and Footnotes

The other style of documentation in wide use is endnotes or footnotes. The difference between these two note forms is that footnotes come at the bottom of the page where the references occur, while endnotes come at the end of the paper. Most authorities consider endnotes quite acceptable. If you do prefer footnotes, however, your word processor may have the ability to place footnotes on the right pages, in acceptable format. You will also need a bibliography at the end of your paper listing your sources in alphabetical order.

One widely accepted authority for note and bibliography style is Kate L. Turabian's *A Manual for Writers.*[10] You may want to consult this work as you write your papers. The list which follows gives examples of notes and bibliographical entries for typical accounting sources.

As with internal documentation, you should introduce your paraphrased or quoted material:

> According to a recent article in *The Wall Street Journal,* many accounting firms find the poor writing skills of their new employees a serious problem.[11]

The introduction to this paraphrase tells generally where the information came from; the note and bibliographical entry give complete information about the source.

NOTES AND BIBLIOGRAPHY

N = Endnote or footnote
B = Bibliographical entry

Book

N   [1]Charles T. Horngren and Walter T. Harrison, *Accounting,* 2nd ed. (Englewood Cliffs, N.J.: Prentice Hall, 1992), p. 403.
B   Horngren, Charles T., and Harrison, Walter T. *Accounting.* 2nd ed. Englewood Cliffs, N.J.: Prentice Hall, 1992.

Article in a Journal

N   [2]Alfred Rappaport, "The Strategic Audit," *Journal of Accountancy* 149 (June 1980): 72.
B   Rappaport, Alfred. "The Strategic Audit," *Journal of Accountancy* 149 (June 1980): pp. 71–77.

APB Opinion

N   [3]Accounting Principles Board, *Disclosure of Lease Commitments by Lessees,* Opinions of the Accounting Principles Board No. 31 (New York: American Institute of Certified Public Accountants, 1973), para. 8.
B   Accounting Principles Board. *Disclosure of Lease Commitments by Lessees.* Opinions of the Accounting Principles Board No. 31. New York: American Institute of Certified Public Accountants, 1979.

FASB—Financial Accounting Standard

N   [4]Financial Accounting Standards Board, *Disclosure of Information About Major Customers: An Amendment of FASB Statement No. 14,* Statement of Financial Accounting Standards No. 30 (Stamford, CT: Financial Accounting Standards Board, 1979), para. 7.

B   Financial Accounting Standards Board. *Disclosure of Information About Major Customers: An Amendment of FASB Statement No. 14.* Statement of Financial Accounting Standards No. 30. Stamford, CT: Financial Accounting Standards Board, 1979.

FASB—Financial Accounting Concept

N   [5]Financial Accounting Standards Board, *Objectives of Financial Reporting by Business Enterprises,* Statement of Financial Accounting Concepts No. 1 (Stamford, CT: Financial Accounting Standards Board, 1978), para. 33.

B   Financial Accounting Standards Board. *Objectives of Financial Reporting by Business Enterprises.* Statement of Financial Accounting Concepts No. 1. Stamford, CT: Financial Accounting Standards Board, 1978.

Primary Source Quoted in Current Text

N   [6]Financial Accounting Standards Board, *Objectives of Financial Reporting by Business Enterprises,* Statement of Financial Accounting Concepts No. 1, as reported in *Accounting Standards: Current Text as of June 1, 1990* (Homewood, IL.: Irwin, 1990), Sec. 1210.

B   Financial Accounting Standards Board. *Objectives of Financial Reporting by Business Enterprises.* Statement of Financial Accounting Concepts No. 1. As reported in *Accounting Standards: Current Text, as of June 1, 1990.* Homewood, IL.: Irwin, 1990.

Legal Citation

N   [7]Aaron v. SEC, 446 U.S. 680(1980).

R   Same form as note.

IRS—Code Section

N   [8]Sec. 6111(a).

R   Internal Revenue Code. Sec. 6111(a).

Federal Register

N   [9]48 Fed. Reg., 1983, p. 52, 579.

R   "Establishment of Sonoma County Green Valley Vitacultural Area, Final Rule." *Federal Register* 48 (Nov. 21, 1983).

EXERCISE

Choose one of the following topics, and narrow it if necessary. (For example, you might select "Careers with the Internal Revenue Service" rather than "Careers in Accounting.") Write a documented research paper on your topic, using the steps discussed in this chapter.

1. History of the Accounting Profession
2. Public- versus Private-Sector Regulation of Accounting
3. Accounting for International Businesses
4. Careers in Accounting
5. Accounting for Pensions
6. Accounting for Oil and Gas Exploration
7. Computers and Accounting
8. Accountants in the F.B.I.

NOTES

1. Financial Accounting Standards Board, *Accounting Standards: Current Text as of June 1, 1990* (Homewood, Ill.: Irwin, 1990).
2. Jane Kubat, ed., *Accountants' Index* (New York: American Institute of Certified Public Accountants).
3. Information on note card quoted from Charles T. Horngren and Walter T. Harrison, *Accounting,* (Englewood Cliffs, N.J.: Prentice-Hall, Inc., 1989), p. 403. Reprinted by permission.
4. John C. Hodges and Mary E. Whitten, *Harbrace College Handbook,* 8th ed. (New York: Harcourt Brace Jovanovich, Inc., 1977), p. 372.
5. Joseph Gibaldi and Walter S. Achtert, *MLA Handbook for Writers of Research Papers,* 2nd ed. (N.Y.: The Modern Language Association of America, 1984), p. 20.
6. Ibid., p. 21.
7. There are many documentation styles in current use. The sample entries in this chapter illustrate acceptable usage, but you may use another acceptable style as long as you're consistent within each paper.
8. *The Chicago Manual of Style,* 13th ed. (Chicago: University of Chicago Press, 1982).
9. *Publication Manual of the American Psychological Association,* 3rd ed. (Washington, D.C.: American Psychological Association, 1983).
10. Kate L. Turabian, *A Manual for Writers of Term Papers, Theses, and Dissertations,* 5th ed. (Chicago: The University of Chicago Press, 1987).
11. Lee Berton, "Take Heart, CPAs: Finally a Story That Doesn't Attack You as Boring," *Wall Street Journal,* May 13, 1987, p. 33.

11

ORAL PRESENTATIONS
Preparation

Speaking before a group, like writing, is often an important part of an accountant's professional responsibilities. Unfortunately, public speaking creates anxiety for many people. If you learn a few strategies for public speaking, however, and practice as often as possible, your fear of these situations will diminish. With guidance and practice comes mastery, and with mastery comes control.

In this chapter and the next one, we'll see that effective oral presentations, like writing, result from a process: preparation, practice, and delivery. This chapter will show you how to prepare for speaking before a group. We'll begin by discussing the first step in any important communication: analyzing the purpose of the presentation and the needs and interests of the audience.

PLANNING THE PRESENTATION: ANALYZING PURPOSE AND AUDIENCE

As with writing, the first step in planning your presentation is to analyze its purpose. Perhaps you need to inform your listeners about the progress you've made on a project, or propose that the decision makers in the group approve a new project. You may be convincing senior management to invest in a new system, or explaining to coworkers how to implement the system already adopted. Remember, too, that no matter what the primary purpose of your presentation, it has an important secondary purpose as well: your desire to impress your listeners as a competent professional.

As you analyze the purpose of your presentation, think also about your audience. How many people will you be speaking to? Will they be a fairly homogenous group, or will you be speaking to people with different degrees of knowledge about your topic and different interests? An important consideration about the audience is which decision makers will be present. In planning your presentation, the needs and interests of these decision makers should be a primary concern.

It will be helpful if you think in advance about the questions your audience will have about your topic, whether or not there will be a formal question-and-answer session as part of the presentation. By anticipating their questions, you can explain your ideas in a way that will be most convincing. Anticipating listeners' questions, and having the information ready to answer them, will also convey to your audience that you are thoroughly prepared, credible and professional.

Throughout the planning and preparation of your speech, think always about your audience: what they know about your topic, what they need to know, what their concerns and interests are, and what their attitudes may be toward your point of view and the information you'll present.

OTHER THINGS TO CONSIDER

In addition to analyzing your purpose and audience, you'll need to be sure about how much time you'll have for your presentation. In addition, find out how you will be speaking to your audience, whether formally or informally, perhaps from your seat in a conference setting.

Yet another consideration is whether to illustrate your main speech with visual aids, such as charts or other graphic material. If you decide to use visual aids, consider the room where the presentation will be made. Will the space and facilities allow you to use the visual aids you prefer? A later section of this chapter will discuss how to prepare effective visual aids. For now, the important point to remember is that you need to start planning your visual aids early.

Finally, budget your time so you can complete the work needed to gather information, compose the speech, make your notes, prepare your visual aids, and practice your presentation. All of these steps take time, particularly if your topic requires much underlying research.

The key to handling all these tasks is to make a schedule with dates for the completion of each step. It's important to plan the work you have to do and budget your time so that you have enough time to accomplish all you must.

GATHERING INFORMATION

The next step in preparing your presentation is to gather the necessary information. Be thorough when you research your topic, so that you can answer any questions your audience may have. Remember: when you are thoroughly prepared, you will seem competent and professional, and your presentation will have an excellent chance of success.

Before you begin the research for your presentation, you may want to review Chapter 2, which discusses how to generate ideas, and Chapter 10, which covers library research.

COMPOSING THE SPEECH

Once you've gathered the information you'll need, you can begin to organize your material into an outline. Keeping in mind the purpose of the speech and the interests of your audience, identify the main points you want to make: *Your speech should contain no more than three to five main points.* These main points, with an introduction and conclusion, will be the outline of your presentation. Let's look now at how you can fill in that outline.

Introduction

Your introduction should do two things: it should get your listeners' attention and preview for them the main points you will cover.

When you plan the opening sentences of your presentation, consider your listeners' point of view. Why should they listen to what you have to say? Will your speech be meaningful to them, perhaps helping them solve a problem or accomplish some goal? What do you and your listeners have in common that would make them interested in your presentation? What makes your topic particularly timely and relevant to your listeners? Questions such as these can help you compose the opening sentences of your presentation to get your audience's attention. Here are a few additional suggestions:

- Begin with an interesting story or example that will introduce your topic.
- Cite a startling statistic.
- Ask a rhetorical question—one that you don't expect your audience to answer but that will start them thinking about the topic.

These are just a few examples of ways to begin your presentation.

After your opening sentences, the next important part of your presentation is a preview of what the speech will cover. If you tell your audience what your main points will be, you'll help them remember what's important as you progress through your presentation.

Body of the Presentation

In the body of your presentation, you present again your main points and develop them in detail. Be specific and concrete: use facts, examples, and, where appropriate, statistics.

As you move from one main point to the next, you can help your listeners remember main ideas with two techniques: internal summaries of what you've already said and clear transitions that lead into the next main topic. For example, you might say something like this:

> *So one advantage of this new system is that it would reduce the time needed to process customer accounts.* (This is an internal summary. We know it's a summary because of the word *so.*) *The second advantage is that the system would provide us with better records for our sales managers.* (This sentence provides a transition into the next major section of the speech and identifies for the listeners the second main point.)

By providing internal summaries and obvious transitions, you can help your listeners remember main ideas as you give your presentation.

Conclusion

The last part of your formal presentation is, of course, your conclusion. Once again, you will help your listeners if you summarize the main ideas you want them to remember. Your presentation will be most effective, however, if you end it with a forceful closing. Here are some suggestions:

- Ask your audience to do something. This call to action may be low key, a request that they consider your recommendation, for example. Or you may want to be more forceful and sometimes even dramatic if you think the topic warrants this approach and if this tone is suitable for your audience.
- Refer again to the opening sentences of your presentation. For example, if you used a story, example, or statistic, suggest how the ideas expressed in your speech relate to these concepts.
- Remind your audience of the benefits they will receive if they follow your recommendations.

If you would like additional help in composing your speech, you will find it useful to review Chapter 3, which covers the principles of coherent organization.

MAKING THE NOTES

Once you have gathered your material and completed the outline for your presentation, you are ready to put your notes in final form—the form from which you will actually speak. Notice that this section does *not* say "Writing your Speech," and for a very good reason. Most experienced speakers find it unnecessary to write down every word they want to say. In fact, having a word-for-word manuscript of your speech could lead you to make two mistakes in your presentation: reading the speech or trying to memorize it. (More about these pitfalls later.)

The most helpful way to prepare your notes is in outline form. You should already have this outline, because you have prepared it as you have gathered your information and organized your materials. Your job now is to put this outline into notes that you can speak from. Here are a few pointers:

- Transfer your outline to either note cards or standard-sized paper. Write large enough that you can see what you've written at a glance.
- Include main points, as well as supporting details and examples.
- Write out the opening sentences for your presentation and the conclusion. (This is the exception to the advice not to write out the speech word for word.)
- Indicate in your notes where you will use your visual aids.
- As you review your notes, underline key phrases, perhaps in a contrasting color of ink. When you make the presentation, these underlined phrases will be reminders of the points you want to make.
- Number your notecards or pages, and clip them together.

When we discuss practicing and delivering your presentation, you will see how notes prepared in this way will help you make a smooth presentation.

PREPARING THE VISUAL AIDS

To appreciate how visual aids can contribute to an effective presentation, consider your audience's point of view.

When people read, they have a number of visual cues to help them identify and remember main ideas. They have titles and headings, paragraph breaks to signal a shift in topic, and often they have graphic illustrations as well. If they need to review something that has already been covered, they have only to turn back the page to see that material again.

Listeners to an oral presentation have none of these visual cues to help them follow the flow of thought, unless the speaker provides them with visual aids. A major advantage of visual aids is that they help your listeners identify and remember main ideas. They offer another advantage as well, because well-constructed, attractive visual aids make the presentation more interesting.

Visual aids appeal to your audience, then, by making your presentation easier to follow and more interesting. But what are the best kinds of aids to use?

To some extent, your choices will depend upon where you'll be speaking. For example, if you are making a classroom presentation, you can prepare handouts, write on the chalkboard, prepare posters and charts, and probably use an overhead projector. In a work setting, you may also have access to more sophisticated equipment, such as video cassette players and projection equipment that can be run by computers.

You may decide to use more than one kind of visual aid. For example, handouts will give your listeners something to take with them to reenforce what you've been saying, especially when you want to give them lengthy or detailed information. But you don't want them reading the handout instead of looking at you when you speak, so it may be a good idea to illustrate your presentation with posters or overhead transparencies and save the handouts for distribution after the presentation.

Let's look more closely at guidelines for preparing visual aids such as posters or overhead transparencies:

- Keep your aids simple. Use key words and phrases, rather than sentences, and limit each aid to no more than about ten lines.
- Be sure your writing is legible. Write clearly, in a dark or bright color so that the writing will be easy to see. Be sure your print is large enough to be seen from the back of the room. If you are using typed or printed material, you may need to enlarge the print on a copier so that it will be readable.
- If possible, use bright colors to make your aids more attractive.
- Your aids should be neat and professional looking. For a transparency, typed or printed material, rather than hand written, is usually preferable. If you use graphic illustrations, a computer with a graphics package will help you achieve a professional appearance.

You can include any information on your visual aid that will help your listeners understand and remember your message, but visual aids are particularly helpful to identify your main points, summarize your recommendations or conclusions, or provide a vivid illustration. You can also summarize statistical information in a table or graph. Yet another technique is to reproduce cartoons to amuse your listeners as you illustrate a point.

Once you have prepared your visual aids and your notes, you are then ready for the next important step in the preparation of your oral presentation: practice.

PRACTICING YOUR PRESENTATION

Practicing your presentation is essential for several reasons. For one thing, the more times you review your speech the more familiar you become with it, so that when you actually speak before your audience you appear knowledgeable and convincing. You will also feel more confident that you have mastered the ideas you want to present. When you practice, especially before other people, you also identify in advance any potential problems that could occur, such as a presentation that is too long or too short for the allotted time.

Here are some strategies that will make your practice time most useful:

- Practice your speech out loud. Pay attention to your voice, posture, and gestures (see Chapter 12 for specific suggestions).
- Time your presentation to check that it is the appropriate length.
- Practice using your visual aids, including any equipment you will be using, such as an overhead projector.
- If possible, practice in the actual room you will be using for your presentation.
- Practice before a live audience, such as friends, family, or coworkers. Ask them to be critical of the content of your speech as well as your delivery.
- If you have access to video equipment, ask someone to make a videotape of your presentation so that you can identify and correct any problems.

Finally, remember these pitfalls to avoid:

Never read or try to memorize your speech!

The only exception to the guideline about memorization is that you may find it helpful to memorize your opening and closing sentences.

CHECKING THE ARRANGEMENTS

For some oral presentations, your preparations will include arranging for a room and equipment. Even if someone else is responsible for these duties, it may be a good idea to double check. And be thorough. For example, be sure that the room will be unlocked in time for the early arrivals at the presentation and that equipment will be delivered and set up in working order.

Check again on these arrangements a little while before your presentation begins. Then if there is some unforeseen problem, such as malfunctioning equipment, you'll have time to correct it.

APPEARANCE AND DRESS

A final consideration in the preparation for your presentation is your own appearance and dress. As in any professional situation, your grooming should be impeccable. The actual clothing you wear will depend to some extent on the situation, but professional styles and colors are almost always preferable. If you are in doubt, it's usually better to err on the side of conservatism.

In summary, thorough preparation for your presentation—your appearance, the arrangements, your visual aids, and the speech itself—will help you ensure good results when you speak before a group.

EXERCISES

Exercise 11-1

Select one of the following topics and prepare a five-minute presentation to give before your class:

- Why I majored in accounting (or in another discipline)
- Tips for studying accounting
- Stereotypes about accountants
- Where I hope to be five years from now
- The users of accounting information

Exercise 11-2

Prepare an oral presentation of the report you wrote for Chapter 9. Assume the audience for the oral presentation is the same as that for the written report. If necessary, condense the material you have included in the written report, prepare additional visual aids, or make any other changes you need to have an effective oral presentation. Reminder: do not read the report to your audience.

Your presentation should be about twenty minutes long.

12

MAKING THE PRESENTATION
Poise and Confidence

The last chapter discussed how to prepare for your presentation before you actually give it: planning, composing, and practice. This chapter will look at the qualities of effective delivery and how you can become an accomplished public speaker.

The effect you should create on your audience is one of poise and confidence. With adequate practice and preparation, you are well on your way to reaching this goal. Let's look now at techniques of actual delivery that contribute to an effective presentation.

EYE CONTACT

One of the secrets of public speaking is eye contact between the speaker and the audience. When you look your listeners in the eye, you help involve them in the topic and help ensure that they listen carefully to what you say.

Begin to establish eye contact when you first stand before your audience: stand straight, smile, and look around the room. Look directly at various individuals at different locations. This initial eye contact should probably last for a total of three or four seconds.

As you begin your actual presentation and progress through it, continue to maintain this eye contact. Hold the eye contact with each person for several seconds, perhaps the length of a complete phrase that you are speaking. Shift the contact from one side of the room to the other, front to back, and at various points in the middle. If your audience is a small one, you may be able to establish eye contact with everyone in the room several times.

Regardless of the size of your audience, though, it is essential that you establish eye contact with one important group of listeners: the decision makers. They will be judging the ideas you present and your effectiveness as a speaker; good eye contact will help you keep their attention. You'll also seem confident and in control of the situation.

You may also find it helpful to look frequently at the listeners that seem most interested and supportive of what you are saying. You can recognize this group by their expressions of interest and attention, perhaps even nods and smiles. Their enthusiasm can give you extra energy and confidence.

When you think about the importance of maintaining good eye contact with the audience, it becomes obvious why you shouldn't read your speech, and why you should be so familiar with your notes that you only glance at them from time to time.

BODY MOVEMENT AND GESTURES

A poised, natural use of your body and gestures will also contribute to an effective presentation. Stand still, with good posture, and look directly at your listeners. Don't move about, except to use your visual aids—for example, to point to something on a chart or to change a transparency on the overhead projector.

A natural, expressive use of your hands is an effective way to emphasize ideas and feelings. For this reason, it is better to place your notes on a table or podium so that your hands are free for gestures.

VOICE

Three elements of your voice will contribute to an effective presentation: pitch, volume, and speed. Pitch refers to how high or low you speak. For most people, their natural pitch is fine and will require no modification for public speaking. A few people need to pitch their voices a little lower than normal, especially if they are nervous when they speak.

Volume and speed may require more attention. The key to speaking in the correct volume is to speak loudly enough so that people in the back of the room can hear you. Be consistent; don't let your voice drop at the ends of sentences, for example, so that your audience misses the last words or must strain to hear you.

When you practice your presentation in advance of your actual presentation, pay particular attention to the speed with which you are speaking. You want to speak slowly enough that you enunciate each word clearly. Some speakers have a tendency to speak more rapidly when they are nervous. If you fall into this category, make a conscious effort to slow down.

MANAGING STAGE FRIGHT

Now that we've introduced the topic of nervousness, let's think for a minute about how to manage what for many speakers is the worst part of public speaking: stage fright. Notice that the heading for this section says, "*managing* stage fright," not "*eliminating*" it. Even the most experienced, effective speakers usually have some stage fright; furthermore, they use this heightened emotion to help them make a more effective presentation. The emotion, if kept in reasonable limits, can give you the extra charge to make an energetic, enthusiastic, and convincing presentation.

But too much stage fright is, of course, counterproductive. Let's look now at some strategies you can use to manage stage fright before and during your presentation.

Well in Advance

One advantage of thorough preparation and practice is that they will help you prevent stage fright. When you know you thoroughly understand your topic, and when you have thought in advance about the questions and interests of your listeners, you will *feel* prepared—and thus competent. A feeling of competence, in turn, will give you confidence in your ability to do a good job.

Actual practice, especially before a live audience, will also increase your confidence.

Just Before You Speak

Two tricks may be helpful in the last few minutes before you are scheduled to speak. The first is to use this time to go over your notes one last time, to be sure your main points, as well as your opening and closing sentences, are fresh in your mind. The second trick is this:

Don't think about how you're feeling!

If you think about being nervous, you'll only increase the feeling. Instead, think about something pleasant that is completely unrelated to your presentation. Perhaps you can think about something nice that you will do later in the day.

During the Presentation

Most speakers find that their stage fright goes away after the first few minutes of their presentation. When you are speaking, look directly at your listeners with poise and confidence: they'll likely reflect these positive feelings back to you. Notice which of your listeners are most interested and receptive to what you're saying, and make frequent eye contact with these people. Their enthusiasm will add to your feelings of confidence and ensure that your presentation is just as effective as you had hoped.

A FINAL WORD

Public speaking may always be a job that fills you with some apprehension. With practice and the mastery of technique, however, you will become much more sure of yourself and your ability to be an effective oral communicator. For that reason, it's a good idea to take advantage of every opportunity to practice your public speaking. The payoff will be greater professional success.

EXERCISES

Exercise 12-1

The more opportunities you have to speak before a group of people, the more confident you'll be of your abilities. With your instructor's approval, make these informal oral presentations:

a. Interview the classmate sitting next to you, and then introduce this person to the rest of the class. You might include in your introduction such information as your neighbor's home town, hobbies, major course of study, and career goals.
b. Explain to the class how to work an accounting problem that was assigned for homework.

Exercise 12-2

Present to your class the presentation prepared for Chapter 11, Exercise 11-1 or 11-2. After the presentation, ask your classmates and instructor to identify what you did well and to suggest ways you could improve.

Exercise 12-3

Have someone videotape a presentation that you make before your class. Then review the tape to identify what you did well and what areas you need to improve.

Exercise 12-4

Learn to be a good listener. When classmates give oral presentations, listen politely and attentively. Then for each speaker, identify

- at least two strengths of the presentation
- two suggestions for improvement

Write your evaluations on 3×5 cards, which you can give to the speakers at the end of class.

Appendix A

WRITING
FOR THE CPA EXAM

One of the more interesting developments to affect the accounting profession in recent years is the AICPA's decision to evaluate writing skills on the CPA exam. Begining in 1994, candidates taking the exam will be explicitly evaluated for the writing skills they show on certain essay questions in three sections of the exam: Auditing, Financial Accounting and Reporting, and Business Law and Professional Responsibilities.

As a matter of fact, however, writing skills have been an important component of the CPA exam for many years. The "Instructions to Candidates" at the beginning of each section of the exam contains this paragraph:[1]

> A CPA is continually confronted with the necessity of expressing opinions and conclusions in written reports in clear, unequivocal language. Although the primary purpose of the examination is to test the candidate's knowledge and application of the subject matter, the ability to organize and present such knowledge in acceptable written language may be considered by the examiners.

The importance of good writing to a candidate's score on an essay should come as no surprise. After all, if graders can't read an essay easily, they're not likely to give full credit for the content.

Just think about the conditions under which the exams are graded. There may be some 420,000 essays graded by about 200 graders during a six-week period. The graders must do their best to grade each essay both quickly and accurately.

Graders of the CPA exam are working under many of the same conditions as those found in the business world: a lot of work to do in a short amount of time. Their job is to determine if the candidates know the answers to the questions asked on the exam. Thus graders appreciate essays that enable them to spot main ideas quickly and easily. They also appreciate sentences that are clear and readable.

Like readers of business documents, graders of the exam want essays to be coherent (main ideas easy to identify, flow of thought easy to follow), concise (no wasted words), and clear (no guesswork about meaning, no distractions by non-standard English). Thus the writing skills emphasized in this book apply to the CPA exam as well as to more common forms of business writing.

STRATEGY FOR WRITING ESSAY QUESTIONS

Answering the essay questions will be easier if you have a strategy for using your time and composing your answer.

Budget Your Time

Managing your time well is a crucial part of your strategy. You may not have as much time as you would like to plan in detail, revise extensively, and then copy your answer over so that you have a perfect paper. But make the time you do have work to your advantage by following the three steps of the writing process: planning, writing, revising.

First, take a few minutes to read the question carefully to be sure that you know what is being asked. You may find it helpful to underline key phrases in the question so that your answer won't overlook something important. Then jot down the main ideas you want to include in your answer. Put numbers by these ideas to arrange them in the most effective order. Planning your answer, the first step in the writing process, should take only three to five minutes.

The next step, writing your answer, should take the bulk of the remaining time. Write as legibly as possible, and write on every other line of your paper to allow room for editing. Write as well as you can, but don't spend much time looking for the perfect word or phrase if it doesn't come quickly. The most important objective is to get the ideas down on paper so you'll get credit for what you know.

Finally, allow at least five minutes to edit your answer. When you edit, check that all words are correctly spelled and that sentences are grammatically correct and clearly constructed. It is acceptable to cross out words and write your revisions in the line above. It is important, however, that your essay remain legible.

Time is a big factor in answering the essay questions on the exam. Make the time you do have work to your advantage by following the three steps of the writing process: planning, writing, revising.

Use the Question
to Organize Your Essay

One way to help graders identify you main ideas is to write in short paragraphs with strong topic sentences. You can use the question itself to suggest the wording of the topic sentences. Sample questions and answers from past exams show how this strategy works. Figures A–1 and A–2 contain two questions from an exam and unofficial answers suggested by the AICPA.[2]

Part *a* of the auditing question (Figure A–1) states this requirement:

> Identify and describe Reed's responsibilities to detect Smith's errors and irregularities.

The answer begins with a variation of the question:

> To satisfy an auditor's responsibilities to detect Smith's errors and irregularities, Reed should:...

The answer then continues with a list of the procedures Reed should follow.

Let's look at part of another question, this time from the business law section of the exam (see Figure A–2):[3]

> Discuss the following assertions, indicating whether such assertions are correct and the reasons therefor.
>   As of March 3, 1989 the risk of loss on the disk drive remained with Xeon.

Here's how the answer to this question begins:

> The assertion that as of March 3, 1989 the risk of loss on the disk drive remained with Xeon is correct.

The remainder of the paragraph then supports this assertion, as shown in Figure A–2.

Use Formatting Techniques
to Make Your Essays Easy
to Read

Good document design will make it easier for graders to read your essays and give you full credit for what you write. While you are obviously limited to what you can accomplish quickly with a paper and pen, formatting techniques such as headings, bullets, and set-off lists will make it easier for graders to spot main ideas and follow your train of thought.

For example, the answer to the auditing question shown in Figure A–1 uses a set-off list with bullets to identify the audit procedures needed to meet various objectives.

QUALITIES OF A GOOD ANSWER

The definition of effective writing provided by the AICPA gives the qualities you should strive for in the essays you write. (See Figure A-3.) According to the AICPA, effective writing meets these criteria:[4]

- Coherent organization
- Conciseness
- Clarity
- Use of standard English
- Responsiveness to the requirements of the question
- Appropriateness to the reader

As you probably realize, these criteria are stressed throughout this book.

When you are studying for the CPA Exam, you may find it helpful to review the chapters in this book that discuss these qualities of effective writing. These chapters would probably be the most useful to you:

Chapter 2–writing appropriately for the reader and responding to the requirements of the question

Chapter 3–organizing for coherence

Chapter 4–writing with a style that is clear and concise

Chapter 5–writing in standard English

Chapter 6–formatting techniques

FIGURE A-1   CPA Exam Essay Question and Answer—Auditing

Question:

Reed, CPA, accepted an engagement to audit the financial statements of Smith Company. Reed's discussions with Smith's new management and the predecessor auditor indicated the possibility that Smith's financial statements may be misstated due to the possible occurrence of errors, irregularities, and illegal acts.

Required:

a. Identify and describe Reed's responsibilities to detect Smith's errors and irregularities. Do **not** identify specific audit procedures.

b. Identify and describe Reed's responsibilities to report Smith's errors and irregularities.

c. Describe Reed's responsibilities to detect Smith's material illegal acts. Do **not** identify specific audit procedures.

d. Describe Reed's additional responsibilities to report on errors, irregularities, and illegal acts if this audit were one to which the requirements of *Government Auditing Standards* apply.

Answer:

a. To satisfy an auditor's responsibilities to detect Smith's errors and irregularities, Reed should

- Assess the risk that Smith's errors and irregularities may cause its financial statements to contain a material misstatement.
- Design the audit to provide reasonable assurance of detecting errors and irregularities that are material to the financial statements.
- Exercise due care in planning, performing, and evaluating the results of audit procedures, and the proper degree of professional skepticism to achieve reasonable assurance that material errors or irregularities will be detected.

b. To satisfy an auditor's responsibilities to report Smith's errors and irregularities, Reed should

- Inform Smith's audit committee, or others having equivalent authority and responsibility, about material irregularities of which Reed becomes aware.
- Express a qualified or an adverse opinion on the financial statements if they are materially affected by an error or irregularity and are not revised.
- Disclaim or qualify an opinion on the financial statements and communicate the findings to the audit committee or the board of directors if the scope of the audit has been restricted concerning a possible irregularity.
- Consider notification of outside parties concerning irregularities in certain circumstances.

c. Reed's responsibilities to detect Smith's illegal acts that have a material and direct effect on Smith's financial statements are the same as that for errors and irregularities.

Reed's responsibilities to detect Smith's illegal acts that have a material and indirect effect on the financial statements are to be aware of the possibility that such illegal acts may have occurred. If specific information comes to Reed's attention that provides evidence concerning the existence of such possible illegal acts, Reed should apply audit procedures specifically directed to ascertaining whether an illegal act has occurred.

d. In an audit to which GAO standards apply, Reed should additionally

- Determine that instances or apparent indications of illegal acts are reported to the funding agency or other specified agency.
- Express positive assurance on whether the items tested were in compliance with applicable laws and regulations.
- Express negative assurance that, except as otherwise noted, nothing come to Reed's attention that caused Reed to believe that the untested items were not in compliance with applicable laws and regulations.

FIGURE A-1 Continued

FIGURE A-2 CPA Exam Essay Question and Answer—Business Law

Question:

On February 20, 1989, Pine, Inc. ordered a specially manufactured computer system consisting of a disk drive and a central processing unit (CPU) from Xeon Corp., a seller of computers and other office equipment. A contract was signed and the total purchase price was paid to Xeon by Pine on the same date. The contract required Pine to pick up the computer system at Xeon's warehouse on March 9, 1989, but was silent as to when risk of loss passed to Pine. The computer system was completed on March 1, 1989, and set aside for Pine's contemplated pickup on March 9, 1989. On March 3, 1989, Pine picked up the CPU. On March 15, 1989, Pine returned the CPU to Xeon for warranty repairs. On March 18, 1989, Xeon mistakenly sold the CPU to Meed, a buyer in the ordinary course of business.

On April 12, 1989, Pine purchased and received delivery of five word processors from Jensen Electronics Corp. for use in its business. The purchase price of the word processors was $15,000. Pine paid $5,000 down and executed an installment purchase note and a security agreement for the balance. The security agreement contained a description of the word processors. Jensen never filed a financing statement. On April 1, 1989, Pine had given its bank a security interest in all of its assets. The bank had immediately perfected its security interest by filing. Pine has defaulted on the installment purchase note.

Required: Discuss the following assertions, indicating whether such assertions are correct and the reasons therefor.

- As of March 3, 1989, the risk of loss on the disk drive remained with Xeon.
- Meed acquired no rights in the CPU as a result of the March 18, 1989, transaction.
- Jensen's security interest in the word processors never attached and therefore Jensen's security interest is not enforceable against Pine.
- Jensen has a superior security interest to Pine's bank.

Answer:

The assertion that as of March 3, 1989 the risk of loss on the disk drive remained with Xeon is correct. Under the UCC Sales Article, if the agreement between the parties is otherwise silent, risk of loss passes to the buyer on the buyer's receipt of the goods if the seller is a merchant. Under the facts, Xeon is a merchant because it sells computer systems. Therefore, the risk of loss remained with Xeon because the disk drive was never received by Pine.

The assertion that Meed acquired no rights in the CPU as a result of the March 18, 1989 transaction is incorrect. Under the UCC Sales Article, any entrusting of possession of goods to a merchant who deals in goods of that kind gives the merchant the power to transfer all rights of the entruster to the buyer in the ordinary course of business. Entrusting includes any delivery and any acquiescence in retention of possession regardless of any condition expressed between the parties to the delivery or acquiescence, and regardless of whether the possessor's disposition of the goods have been such as to be larcenous under the criminal law. For the merchant to acquire the power to transfer ownership and title, the entruster must be the rightful owner. Under the facts of this case, Pine had title at the time the CPU was returned to Xeon for repairs and this constituted an entrusting that gave Xeon the power to transfer all of Pine's rights in the CPU to Meed.

The assertion that Jensen's security interest in the word processors never attached and therefore Jensen's security interest is not enforceable against Pine with respect to the word processors is incorrect. A security interest in collateral will attach if: the collateral is in the possession of the secured party under an agreement, or the debtor has signed a security agreement that contains a description of the collateral; the secured party has given value; and the debtor has rights in the collateral. Based on the facts, Jensen's security interest attached on April 12, 1989, when Jensen sold and Pine received the word processors and Jensen received a security agreement executed by Pine that described the word processors. On attachment, Jensen's security interest became enforceable against Pine.

The assertion that Jensen has a superior security interest to Pine's bank is incorrect. Although Jensen has a purchase money security interest to the extent the security interest is taken by Jensen to secure the purchase price, Jensen's security interest will not be perfected by attachment alone. Jensen must file a financing statement to perfect its security interest because the collateral involved is goods used for business purposes and not consumer goods. Therefore, Jensen had an unperfected security interest in the word processors and the bank obtained a superior security interest by perfecting.

FIGURE A-2 Continued

FIGURE A-3 The AICPA's Definition of Writing Skills

DEFINITION OF WRITING SKILLS

Answers to selected essay quesitons will be used to assess a candidate's writing skills. Effective writing skills include the following characteristics:

- Coherent organization
- Conciseness
- Clarity
- Use of standard English
- Responsiveness to the requirements of the question
- Appropriateness to the reader

The following are general descriptions of the six characteristics of writing skills.

1. *Coherent organization.* Responses should be organized so that ideas are arranged logically and the flow of thought is easy to follow. Generally, knowledge is best expressed by using short paragraphs composed of short sentences. Moreover, short paragraphs, each limited to the development of one principal idea, can better emphasize the main points in the answer. Each principal idea should be placed in the first sentence of the paragraph, followed by supporting concepts and examples.

2. *Conciseness.* Conciseness requires that candidates present complete thoughts in as few words as possible, while ensuring that important points are covered adequately. Short sentences and simple wording also contribute to concise writing.

3. *Clarity.* A clearly written response prevents uncertainty concerning the candidate's meaning or reasoning. Clarity involves using words with specific and precise meaning, including proper technical terminology. Well-constructed sentences also contribute to clarity.

4. *Use of standard English.* Responses should be written using standard English. *The Business Writer's Handbook*[5] describes standard English as follows:

> There are two broad varieties of written English: standard and nonstandard. These varieties are determined through usage by those who write in the English language. Standard English...is used to carry on the daily business of the nation. It is the language of business, industry, government, education, and the professions. Standard English is characterized by exacting standards of punctuation and capitalization, by accurate spelling, by exact diction, by an expressive vocabulary, and by knowledgeable usage choices.

5. *Responsiveness to the requirements of the question.* Answers should directly address the requirements of the question and demonstrate the candidate's awareness of the purpose of the writing task. Responses should not be broad expositions on the general subject matter.

6. *Appropriateness for the reader.* Writing that is appropriate for the reader takes into account the reader's background, knowledge of the subject, interests, and concerns. The requirements of some essay questions may ask candidates to prepare a written document for a certain reader, such as an engagement memorandum for a CPA's client. When the intended reader is not specified, the candidate should assume the intended reader is a knowledgeable CPA.

FIGURE A-3 Continued

NOTES

1. American Institute of Certified Public Accountants, *Uniform CPA Examination, May 1989; Questions and Unofficial Answers* (New York: American Institute of Certified Public Accountants, 1989), p. 1.
2. Ibid., pp. 36, 68.
3. Ibid., pp. 47, 71.
4. American Institute of Certified Public Accountants, "Definition of Writing Skills" (New York: American Institute of Certified Public Accountants, 1990).
5. Charles T. Brusaw, Gerald J. Alred, and Walter E. Oliu, *the Business Writers' Handbook,* Third Edition (New York: St. Martin's Press, 1987), p. 220.

Appendix B

WRITING FOR PUBLICATION

Sometimes accountants write articles for publication in professional journals such as the *Journal of Accountancy, The CPA Journal,* or *Management Accounting.* The techniques discussed in this book apply to writing articles, but you'll need to consider some additional pointers when you write for publication.

Start by considering the topic of the article you wish to write. Most likely, your article will be based on some of your own experiences in practice. You might also write a position paper or essay on some controversial issue currently under discussion within the profession.

Once you have chosen a topic, visit a good library to find out what else has been published about that subject. This research will help you in several ways:

1. You will find out what has been published recently on your topic, so your article will not repeat what has already been done.
2. You will find out what issues or approaches are of current interest in the profession.
3. You may find references that you can use in your article to support your position. Alternatively, you may find positions taken by other people that you want to refute.

Once you have your material together and have a pretty good idea of what you want to say, you'll need to consider carefully the journal to which you'll submit the article. This step in preparing your article is important because it will enable you to prepare so that it has the best chance of acceptance for publication. Consider these questions about your targeted journal:

1. Who are the readers of the journal? What are their interests and concerns?
2. What type of articles does this journal publish? Some publications prefer articles that emphasize empirical research and statistics, while others are oriented more toward practice.
3. What format, organization, and length do the journal's editors prefer? You can learn this information either from a statement of editorial policy or by studying the articles already published.
4. What writing style do the editors prefer? Articles in professional accounting journals may be written in a serious, scholarly style or a light, conversational one. All journals, however, prefer prose that is clear, readable, and concise, a style that avoids accounting jargon as much as possible.

After you analyze the journal and plan your article, draft and revise your article according to the guidelines discussed in this book. Then when you feel reasonably satisfied with the article, ask colleagues to critique it. People who have themselves successfully published may be particularly helpful.

After all this preparation, your article should have a good chance of acceptance for publication. However, remember to be prepared for the possibility that your article will be rejected by the first journal you send it to.

If your article is rejected, turn it around and send it somewhere else. Be sure, though, to revise it to suit the readers and editorial policies of the new journal.

INDEX

A

Abstract writing, 58–60
Accountant's Index, 175
Accounting Standards: Current Text,
  175
Acronyms, 54
Active voice, 60–62
Adelberg, Arthur, 3
Agreement
  pronoun-antecedent, 77–78
  subject-verb, 76–77
AICPA, 102, 196
  definition of writing skills, 202
American Accounting Association, 1,
  3
Antecedents, 77–78
Apostrophes, rules for, 80–81
Appeals to authority, 35
Appendices to report, 152
Audience, analyzing, 184–185

B

Bibliography, 153, 166, 175–176,
  181–182
Body movement, 193
Brainstorming, 16

C

Clarity, 5, 54–65, 94–99, 103, 135, 137, 202
Clauses, 74–75, 80, 82, 84
Coherent writing, 4–5, 24–45
  on CPA exam, 197, 202
  discussion questions and essays, 36–41
  in letters, 102–103
  in memo, 130–131
  in paragraphs, 32–35
  pronouns to achieve, 30–31
  in reports, 149
  summary sentences, using, 25–26
  transitions for, 27–31
  unity, writing with, 24–25
Colons, 83–84
Commas, 81–83
Comma splices, 74–75
Complex-deductive paragraph, 33–34, 36–37
Computer, writing at, 21–22
  brainstorming and, 16
  document design, 99
  editing for style, 65–66
  error checking with, 86
  outlining program, 16, 17
  revision and, 19–20
Conciseness, 5, 47–53, 103, 137, 202
Conclusions, 26, 38, 102–103, 130–131, 152, 165, 187